UNITED NATIONS CONFERENCE ON TRADE AND DEVELOPMENT

TNCs and the Removal of Textiles and Clothing Quotas

UNITED NATIONS
New York and Geneva, 2005

Note

UNCTAD serves as the focal point within the United Nations Secretariat for all matters related to foreign direct investment and transnational corporations. In the past, the Programme on Transnational Corporations was carried out by the United Nations Centre on Transnational Corporations (1975 1992) and the Transnational Corporations and Management Division of the United Nations Department of Economic and Social Development (1992 1993). In 1993, the Programme was transferred to the United Nations Conference on Trade and Development. UNCTAD seeks to further the understanding of the nature of transnational corporations and their contribution to development and to create an enabling environment for international investment and enterprise development. UNCTAD's work is carried out through intergovernmental deliberations, research and analysis, technical assistance activities, seminars, workshops and conferences.

The term "country" as used in this study also refers, as appropriate, to territories or areas; the designations employed and the presentation of the material do not imply the expression of any opinion whatsoever on the part of the Secretariat of the United Nations concerning the legal status of any country, territory, city or area or of its authorities, or concerning the delimitation of its frontiers or boundaries. In addition, the designations of country groups are intended solely for statistical or analytical convenience and do not necessarily express a judgement about the stage of development reached by a particular country or area in the development process.

The material contained in this study may be freely quoted with appropriate acknowledgement.

UNCTAD/ITE/IIA/2005/1

UNITED NATIONS PUBLICATION
Sales No. E.05.II.D.20
ISBN 92-1-112680-0
ISSN 1818-1465

UN2

TD/UNCTAD/ITE/IIA/2005/1

Foreword

In recent decades, exports of textiles and clothing have been among the most dynamic segments of world trade, and developing countries have accounted for a rising share of this growth. Historically, textiles and clothing were the entry point and backbone of economic development and industrialization for many countries before they moved up the value chain. Hence the great interest in this area of economic activity.

The Multifibre Arrangement in 1974, through its quotas, often effectively limited opportunities for producers to expand their exports to developed countries. They subsequently shifted some of their production activities to locations less constrained by quota limitations or enjoying preferential market access. Foreign affiliates, notably of companies headquartered in Asia, now account for a substantial share of textiles and clothing exports from developing countries.

As part of the Uruguay Round of Multilateral Trade Negotiations, the Multifibre Arrangement was replaced by the Agreement on Textiles and Clothing, which stipulated the phasing out of all quota restrictions over a 10-year transition period ending 1 January 2005. The end of this agreement contributes to the "upholding and safeguarding of an open, non-discriminatory, predictable, rule-based, and equitable multilateral trading system", an objective reaffirmed in the São Paulo Consensus adopted at UNCTAD XI in June 2004.

This study explores the development implications of the phasing out of quotas for FDI in and exports from developing countries. The role of foreign-owned production in the textiles and clothing value chain merits attention. This study takes stock of the available knowledge and explores possible implications for selected developing countries that are highly dependent on textiles and clothing as a source of export revenue.

Carlos Fortin
Officer-in-Charge of UNCTAD

Geneva, May 2005

Acknowledgements

This Report is part of a new Series of Current Studies on FDI and Development published by UNCTAD with a view to contribute to a better understanding of transnational corporations and their activities, and their impact on development. The series also aims at stimulating discussion and further research on the subjects addressed.

The study was prepared under the guidance of Anne Miroux and Karl P. Sauvant. It is based on a manuscript prepared by Richard P. Appelbaum. Torbjörn Fredriksson was responsible for producing the volume.

The text reflects comments and other inputs from Rory Allan, Marc Bachetta, Jennifer Bair, Nelly Berthault, Americo Beviglia-Zampetti, Peter Brimble, Dinora Diaz, Gary Gereffi, Peter Gibbon, Vishwas Govitrikar, Michiko Hayashi, Michael Herrmann, Henri Laurencin, Guoyong Liang, Alfredo Milian, Michael Mortimore, Hildegunn Kyvik Nordås, Arianna Rossi, Dean Spinanger and Zbigniew Zimny. The University of California Institute for Labor and Employment provided partial funding for the work by Richard P. Appelbaum. Joe Conti and Francesca de Giuli provided research assistance.

The text was copy-edited by Talvi Laev, Lynda Piscopo provided secretarial assistance and desktop publishing was done by Teresita Sabico.

Contents

                                                                                                Page

Foreword iii

Acknowledgements iv

List of Figures and Tables vii

Executive Summary viii

I.   Introduction 1

II.   Apparel and textile exports from developing economies 3

      A.   Trade patterns 3
      B.   The changing geography of apparel sourcing 5

III. Large retailers and foreign producers 7

      A.   A value chain driven by large retailers 7
      B.   The emergence of TNC producers in apparel and textiles 8

IV.   Trade arrangements affecting the location of textiles and clothing production 13

      A.   The Multifibre Arrangement 13
      B.   The Agreement on Textiles and Clothing 14
      C.   Quotas and tariffs in preferential trade agreements 15
      D.   Factors mitigating the effects of quota removal 16

V.   The impact of quota elimination 19

VI.   Conclusions and policy options 27

      A.   The impact of quota phase-out 27
      B.   How the emergence of large producers affects policy making 28
      C.   National economic policies 28
      D.   Industry-level policies 30

Annex: Case Studies 31

      1.   Africa 33
           a.   South Africa 33
           b.   Lesotho 34
           c.   Madagascar 35
           d.   Kenya 35
           e.   Mauritius 36
           f.   Tunisia 37

Page

2.   Latin America and the Caribbean 37
         a.   Mexico.. 38
         b.   Dominican Republic... 40
         c.   Guatemala 41
         d.   Honduras 41

3.   Asia 42
         a.   Bangladesh... 42
         b.   Nepal 44
         c.   India.. 45
         d.   Pakistan 46
         e.   Sri Lanka.. 46
         f.   Cambodia 48

Notes **50**

References **55**

Selected UNCTAD publications on FDI and TNCs **61**

Questionnaire... **71**

List of Figures and Tables

Figure

1. Labour costs in the apparel industry, selected economies, 2000 1

Tables

1. The 20 largest apparel exporters, 2003 3
2. 20 economies with high dependence on apparel exports, 2003 4
3. 20 largest textile exporters, 2003 4
4. 20 economies with high dependence on textiles exports, 2003 5
5. Exporters that are highly dependent on exports of apparel and textiles, 2003 5
6. FDI projects in textiles and clothing manufacturing, 2002–2004,
   by host region... 9
7. FDI projects in textiles and clothing manufacturing, 2002–2004,
   by host economy... 9
8. FDI projects in textiles and clothing manufacturing, 2002–2004,
   by source region... 10
9. Top 20 investors in FDI projects in textiles and clothing manufacturing,
   2002–2004.. 10
10. Stages of integration of textiles and apparel into GATT under ATC, 1995–2005 14
11. Regional differences in quota constraints of US apparel imports, 2001 15
12. US apparel imports, by source and risk level, 2002–2005.. 21
13. Largest exporters of textiles and clothing, China, 2003.. 22
14. Number of FDI projects in textiles and clothing in China, 2002–2004,
    by source economy.. 23
15. Lesotho: largest foreign affiliates in garments and footwear, 2002................................... 34
16. Share of total apparel exports from CBI countries to the United States that
    fall under the CBTPA shared production arrangements, 2001 38
17. Textile and apparel firms in Honduras, 2003.. 42

Explanatory notes

The following symbols are used in the tables:

Two dots (..) indicate that data are not available or are not separately reported. Rows in tables have been omitted in cases where no data are available for any of the elements in the row.

A dash (-) indicates that the item is equal to zero or its value is negligible.

A blank in a table indicates that the item is not applicable.

A slash (/) between dates representing years (e.g. 1994/1995) indicates a financial year.

Use of a dash (–) between dates representing years (e.g. 1994–1995) signifies the full period involved, including the beginning and end years.

References to "dollars" ($) are to United States dollars, unless otherwise indicated.

Annual rates of growth or change refer to annual compound rates, unless otherwise stated.

Because of rounding, details and percentages in tables do not necessarily add up to totals.

Executive Summary

For developing countries, the textiles and clothing industries have traditionally been an important gateway to industrialization and increased exports. With the expiration of the Agreement on Textiles and Clothing, the quota system originally set up through the Multifibre Arrangement was phased out. This has important implications for the allocation of export-oriented production and is likely to affect in various ways a large number of developing countries that rely heavily on such exports.

Drawing on a wide range of studies as well as on original research, this volume shows that transnational corporations (TNCs) are likely to play a critical role in determining the future global production structure in these industries. First, the sourcing strategies of a small number of very large retailing companies (based in the United States, Europe and Japan) place stringent requirements on the locations in which textiles and clothes will be produced. Second, the investment strategies of large transnational producers (mostly based in East Asia) will also affect the final outcome. Foreign affiliates of such developing-country TNCs already account for the bulk of exports from many developing economies. The growing role of TNC producers is still not well understood, and more research is needed on their strategies and the impact of their international investments. As TNCs become more important at the production stage, their bargaining power increases vis-à-vis retailers in developed economies.

With the removal of quotas, sourcing and investment decisions are affected more by economic fundamentals. But low labour costs alone will not be sufficient to attract investment. There is likely to be more consolidation of production into larger factories in a smaller number of locations. China and India are likely to be in a particularly strong position in this new geography of production, but various factors may also work against too much consolidation. Proximity to markets continues to play an important role for some product categories, and some producers have signalled that they will retain several production bases in order not to become too dependent on a single source country. Moreover, various trade policy measures also influence sourcing and investment decisions. Data on foreign direct investment (FDI) projects in textiles and clothing manufacturing show that China, Bulgaria, the United States, Hungary, Brazil and India attracted the largest number of such projects in 2002–2004.

The removal of quotas generally means intensified competition for FDI in textiles and clothing. To become or stay competitive as host locations, countries will need to develop their ability to move away from simple assembly to "full-package" production and eventually original brand manufacture. But replicating the success of East Asia will be difficult. Key policy areas in this regard include identification of specialized niches; skills training and technological upgrading; investment in information technology; improvement of infrastructure such as ports and export processing zones; and leveraging of existing tariff preferences in the global trading system. Moreover, investment promotion agencies may identify some of the major transnational producers as key addresses for future marketing activities.

I. Introduction

Global trade in apparel and textiles has increased 60-fold during the past 40 years and in 2003 represented about 5.4% of world merchandise exports. The more labour-intensive apparel exports have grown more rapidly than textile exports, and today apparel accounts for more than half (57%) of the total. Forty years ago, the industrialized countries dominated global exports in this area. Today, developing countries produce half of the world's textile exports and nearly three quarters of world apparel exports.

While the globalization of apparel production has been driven by many factors, chief among these are (1) labour costs and (2) the quota system established by the Multifibre Arrangement (MFA) in 1974. Concerning the former, the difference in apparel labour costs between countries plays a significant role in the global apparel production system (Figure 1). Concerning the latter, quotas ceased to be a significant factor on 1 January 2005. Meanwhile, various other trade policy arrangements continue to affect the allocation of production and exports

in these industries. It is therefore important to consider how production patterns are likely to change with the phasing out of quotas. Quota removal generally means intensified competition among suppliers, and low labour costs alone will not be sufficient to attract production of textiles and clothing. Many countries need to develop their ability to move away from simple assembly to "full-package" production and eventually original brand manufacture in order to stay or become competitive.

Transnational corporations (TNCs) play an increasingly important role in the global distribution and production of apparel and textiles. Large retailing firms exert a strong influence on where imported products are sourced. Moreover, in many developing countries, foreign affiliates of TNCs account for a considerable – and sometimes dominant – share of total production and exports. Hence the need to assess how the phasing out of quotas will affect different countries, and what policy interventions are needed to meet emerging challenges.

Figure 1. Labour costs in the apparel industry, selected economies, 2000
(Average hourly wages in US dollars)

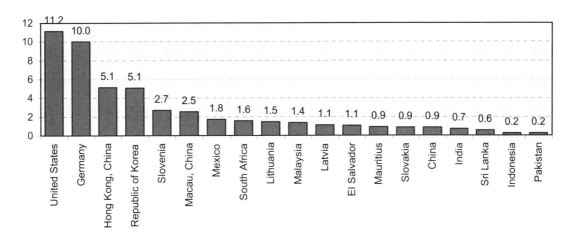

Source: ILO 2003; EU 2003a: 11.

Note: The most recent year for which there are consistent estimates is 2000. Estimates for China, India, Malaysia and Sri Lanka were derived from EU (2003b: 11); all other figures were derived from the ILO online Laborsta database, Table 5B. Figures for Hong Kong (China) and Pakistan are estimated as 84% of textile wages. Apparel and textile figures for El Salvador, Indonesia and South Africa were not separated in the ILO database. Wage rates for least developed countries (LDCs) are not available from the ILO or in a reliable form, but clearly they are at the bottom of the scale.

II. Apparel and textile exports from developing economies

A. Trade patterns

The apparel and textile industries have offered important opportunities for countries to start industrializing their economies and diversify away from commodity dependence. They played an especially important role in the export-oriented development of East Asia – initially in Hong Kong (China), Singapore, Taiwan Province of China, the Republic of Korea and Malaysia, and more recently in China, Indonesia, Thailand and Viet Nam. Moreover, the economic performance of the apparel and textiles industries has had socioeconomic implications related to employment opportunities for women, the development of small- and medium-sized enterprises (SMEs) and spillovers into the informal sector (UNCTAD 2004a).

In 2003, global apparel and textile exports totalled about $421 billion. More than 140 economies produce apparel and textiles for export, and many are highly dependent on these exports for employment and foreign exchange. Although many countries are importers of apparel and textiles, in reality developing-country exports of these products go to two principal markets – the United States and the European Union (EU). The EU was the world's largest apparel and textiles importer in 2003 at $154 billion, with the United States second at $90 billion. However, a large proportion of EU apparel imports is sourced from among EU members. Excluding such imports, the United States is the world's largest single market, some 11% larger than the EU.

Global apparel exports totalled $236 billion in 2003. A handful of countries dominate the global apparel export market. The 20 largest exporters (counting the EU as a single entity, and including intra-EU transactions) accounted for 87% of global apparel exports; three (the EU, China and Hong Kong (China)) accounted for more than half (58%) (Table 1).[1] Turkey (4.2%), Mexico (3.1%) and India (2.8%) all had larger exports than the United States in 2003.

Many developing countries are highly dependent on apparel exports, which may account for a significant share of their total industrial goods export earnings. The largest apparel exporters are not necessarily the most dependent on apparel exports, however. Table 2 shows 20 economies for which apparel exports comprised a large share of total merchandise exports in 2003. In eight of these economies, apparel exports constituted about half or more of total merchandise exports. Among the least developed countries (LDCs) there were four examples: Cambodia (84%), Haiti (82%), Bangladesh (76%) and Lesotho (65%).

Table 1. The 20 largest apparel exporters, 2003
(Million dollars and percentage)

Economy	1990	2003	Total 2003 (%)
World	*108,408*	*235,825*	*100.0*
EU-15	39,968	60,721	25.7
China	9,669	52,162	22.1
China, Hong Kong SAR	15,406	23,246	9.9
Turkey	3,331	9,963	4.2
Mexico	89	7,343	3.1
India	2,533	6,641	2.8
United States	2,569	5,549	2.4
Indonesia	1,666	4,151	1.8
Romania	429	4,069	1.7
Thailand	2,828	3,663	1.6
Rep. of Korea	8,020	3,647	1.5
Bangladesh	643	3,635	1.5
Pakistan	1,028	2,901	1.2
Morocco	722	2,847	1.2
Tunisia	1,126	2,722	1.2
Sri Lanka	643	2,516	1.1
Viet Nam[a]	215	2,490	1.1
Philippines	681	2,287	1.0
Taiwan Province of China	4,023	2,114	0.9
Poland	365	2,074	0.9

Source: UNCTAD.

[a]   Includes estimates by the UNCTAD secretariat.

Textile production is more capital-intensive than apparel production. Here, therefore, developing countries account for a smaller share of world exports. Global textile exports reached $186 billion in 2003 (Table 3). The EU was the largest exporter, accounting for about a third of the total (15% excluding intra-EU trade), followed by China (15%), Hong Kong (China) (7%), the United States (6%) and the Republic of Korea (6%).

Dependence on textile exports is less marked (Table 4). With the exception of Pakistan, for which nearly half of all merchandise exports consisted of textiles in 2003, in no country did textiles comprise more than a fifth of total merchandise exports. Nepal (16%), one of two LDCs in Table 4, was the second most dependent on textiles, followed by Macao (China) (12%), Turkey (11%) and India (11%).

In 2003, apparel and textile exports combined accounted for more than 80% of total merchandise exports in Cambodia, Haiti, Bangladesh and Macao (China); 70% in Pakistan and Lesotho; and 50% to 60% in Mauritius, Sri Lanka, Tokelau and Nepal (Table 5). In another five countries, such exports accounted for more than a third of total merchandise exports.

Table 2. 20 economies with high dependence on apparel exports, 2003
(Million dollars and percentage)

Economy	Total amount	Share in economy's total merchandise exports
World	235,825	3.2
Cambodia	1,493	84.3
Haiti[a]	284	82.2
Northern Mariana Islands[a]	903	76.4
Bangladesh	3,635	75.9
China, Macao SAR	1,834	71.0
Lesotho[a]	314	65.3
Mauritius	986	52.9
Sri Lanka	2,516	51.7
Cape Verde[a]	7	49.7
Lao People's Dem. Rep.[a]	157	41.6
Dominican Republic[a]	432	41.5
Tokelau[a]	0.053	40.5
Tunisia	2,722	37.0
Nepal	226	34.6
Albania	153	34.3
Morocco	2,847	32.4
Maldives	36	32.0
Madagascar	238	31.1
Macedonia, TFYR	409	30.0
Fiji	135	26.8

Source: UNCTAD.
[a] 1990 includes estimates by the UNCTAD secretariat.

Table 3. The 20 largest textile exporters, 2003
(Million dollars and percentage)

Economy	1990	2003	2003 % total
World	112,666	185,596	100.0
EU-15	50,850	59,906	32.3
China	7,219	27,176	14.6
China, Hong Kong SAR	8,224	13,093	7.1
United States	5,061	10,884	5.9
Republic of Korea	6,084	10,777	5.8
Taiwan Province of China	6,219	9,392	5.1
India	2,180	6,856	3.7
Japan	5,850	6,426	3.5
Pakistan	2,663	6,030	3.2
Turkey	1,440	5,263	2.8
Indonesia	1,264	2,940	1.6
Canada	687	2,264	1.2
Thailand	931	2,195	1.2
Mexico	342	2,097	1.1
Czech Republic	...	1,727	0.9
Switzerland	2,569	1,499	0.8
Poland	270	1,144	0.6
Brazil	799	1,120	0.6
Malaysia	381	1,022	0.6
Iran[a]	529	793	0.4

Source: UNCTAD.
[a] 1990 includes estimates by the UNCTAD secretariat.
... Not available.

Table 4. 20 economies with high dependence on textiles exports, 2003
(Million dollars and percentage)

Economy	Total amount	Share in economy's total merchandise exports
World	*185,596*	*3.2*
Pakistan	6,030	47.5
Nepal	107	16.4
Macao (china)	303	11.7
Turkey	5,263	11.1
India	6,856	10.9
Bangladesh	351	7.3
Taiwan Province of China	9,392	6.2
China	27,176	6.2
Hong Kong (China)	13,093	5.7
Korea, Republic of	10,777	5.6
Latvia	156	5.4
Indonesia	2,940	4.8
Egypt	278	4.5
Belarus	449	4.5
Lithuania	288	4.0
Estonia	220	3.9
Sri Lanka	161	3.3
Tunisia	269	3.7
Czech Republic	1,727	3.5
Bulgaria	254	3.4

Source: UNCTAD.

Table 5. Exporters that are highly dependent on exports of apparel and textiles, 2003[a]
(Percentage share of total merchandise exports)

Economy	Apparel	Textiles	Total
Cambodia	84.3	1.0	85.3
Haiti[a]	82.2	1.9	84.1
Bangladesh	75.9	7.3	83.3
China, Macao SAR	71.0	11.7	82.8
Pakistan	22.9	47.5	70.3
Lesotho[a]	65.3	5.0	70.3
Mauritius	52.9	4.1	57.1
Sri Lanka	51.7	3.3	55.0
Tokelau[a]	13.0	40.5	53.4
Nepal	34.6	16.4	51.0
Dominican Republica	41.5	1.7	43.3
Lao People's Dem. Rep.[a]	41.6	0.2	41.8
Tunisia	37.0	3.7	40.7
Albania	34.3	0.3	34.6
Morocco	32.4	1.5	33.9
FYR Macedonia	30.0	3.1	33.1
Madagascar	31.1	1.4	32.5
Turkey	21.1	11.1	32.2
Maldives	32.0	0.0	32.0
Fiji	26.8	1.2	28.0

Source: UNCTAD.
[a] Includes estimates by the UNCTAD secretariat.

B.   The changing geography of apparel sourcing[2]

The number of countries with significant exports of apparel has increased sharply over time. In 1980, economies whose exports exceeded $1 billion included only Hong Kong (China), Taiwan Province of China and the Republic of Korea, along with China and the United States. A decade later, the list also included India, Indonesia, Malaysia, Pakistan, the Philippines, Thailand, Turkey (which had emerged as the world's fifth-largest apparel exporter) and Tunisia. By 2003, the list had been extended with yet other entrants, such as Bangladesh, Mexico, Sri Lanka and several countries of Central and Eastern Europe (CEE).

With regard to US apparel imports since 1990,[3] North-East Asia[4] experienced a relative decline in importance as a source region between 1990 and 2003, from 54% of all imports to 29%. China maintained a fairly constant share of around 13% to 17%, while the other North-East Asian economies recorded a steady decline, from 40% to 13% of US imports. During the same period, Mexico saw its share of US apparel imports increase from 4% to 14% in 2000 and then fall back to 11% in 2003. Exports by the Caribbean Basin Initiative countries fared somewhat better, growing from 8% in 1990 to 16% in 2003.[5]

European imports show a similar pattern, with Hong Kong (China) and China now the leading Asian exporters. Prominent new exporters to Europe include Turkey, Tunisia, Morocco and several CEE countries. While Tunisia and Morocco engage mainly in assembly, the other countries are capable of full-package production.

Japan, once a major exporter of apparel and textiles, is now the world's fourth largest import market (after the United States, the EU and Hong Kong (China)).[6] In 2003, thanks to a recovering economy, textile and clothing imports increased by 11%; China accounted for fully 82% of Japan's clothing imports in that year and 45% of its textile imports (TI 2004). There are a number of reasons for China's prominent role in Japan's textile and apparel imports, including inflows of Japanese FDI, geographic proximity to Japan and, not least, the absence of quotas (TI 2004).

Although the United States and the EU both rely heavily on imports from Asia, there is clearly a strong regional component to sourcing, with the United States importing from Mexico, Central America and the Caribbean, Europe from CEE and North Africa, and Japan from China. Moreover, Asian exporters provide full-package production, while Mexico, Central America, the Caribbean, CEE and northern Africa are primarily involved in assembly activities, namely sewing textiles from the United States and the EU into garments. Partly owing to rules of origin requirements in preferential trade agreements, such lower-value-added activities offer less scope for industrial upgrading and economic development.

III. Large retailers and foreign producers

Apparel and textile production are typical examples of global "buyer-driven" commodity chains

"in which large retailers, marketers and branded manufacturers play the pivotal roles in setting up decentralized production networks in a variety of exporting countries, typically located in developing countries. This pattern of trade-led industrialization has become common in labour-intensive, consumer-goods industries such as garments, footwear, toys, handicrafts and consumer electronics. Tiered networks of third-world contractors that make finished goods for foreign buyers carry out production. Large retailers or marketers that order the goods supply the specifications" (Gereffi and Memedovic 2003: 3).

Global textile and apparel production can be seen as consisting of a series of intersecting networks organized around five principal activities: raw material supply, component provision, production networks, export channels and marketing networks (Appelbaum and Gereffi 1994). Barriers to entry are low on the production side, at least compared with more complex industries like electronics or automobiles, but higher at the retail end of the value chain. For a country to benefit from these networks, it is essential to link up with the major lead firms in the industry. Increasingly these are found at the retailing and designing end of the value chain – activities that entail product design, new technologies, brand names or creating consumer demand. While simple assembly is a source of jobs and therefore can play an important role in developing economies, for many countries it no longer represents an obvious path to higher-value-added activities.

East Asian producers have been able to move up from "captive networks" (in which producers are limited to the assembly of cut fabric following detailed instructions) into "relational value chains" entailing "more complex forms of coordination, knowledge exchange, and supplier autonomy" and permitting full-package production (Gereffi, Humphrey and Sturgeon 2003: 12). There is a significant debate regarding whether East Asia's success can be replicated in a world increasingly dominated by large TNC retailers and producers.

A. A value chain driven by large retailers

One of the principal changes in global apparel commodity production has been the growing economic power of retailers based predominantly in developed countries. Large retailing firms exert a great deal of control over prices and sourcing locations, both through the price pressures they can exert on the independent labels they carry and through their growing volume of private-label production (now estimated to encompass as much as one third of all US retail apparel sales). The world's 40 largest retailers had nearly $1.3 trillion in total revenues in 2001. Of the top 40, 12 were based in the United States and accounted for 43% of total revenues. Almost all of the remaining ones were from the EU (accounting for 46%). The only Asian firms in the top 40 were five Japanese retailers (accounting for the remaining 11%). Some of these firms, such as Wal-Mart (with 1.4 million employees) and Pinault-Printemps Redoute, feature among the top 100 TNCs in the world (UNCTAD 2004c).[7]

In relation to these trends, there has since the mid-1980s been a move towards "lean retailing", particularly in the United States but also in Europe and Japan. Traditionally, apparel-producing firms and retailers were relatively independent of one another. Led by Wal-Mart and other large US firms, and enabled by technological changes that permitted a high degree of data sharing and other electronic interchange, retailers have increasingly brought their suppliers under more direct control, requiring them to "implement information technologies for exchanging sales data, adopt standards for product labelling, and use modern methods of material handling that assured customers a variety of products at low prices" (Abernathy et al. 1999: 3). As Nordås (2004: 4) notes, "lean retailers in the United States typically replenish their stores on a weekly basis".

This favours producers that can provide quick turn-around – either because they are geographically close to their principal markets (e.g. Mexico, Central America and the Caribbean countries to the United States; Turkey and CEE to the EU) or because they can quickly and efficiently organize the entire supply chain. The latter favours producers in Hong Kong (China), Taiwan Province of China and the Republic of Korea that are well positioned to manage triangle manufacturing[8] in the global apparel industry. As was noted in a study of firms from Taiwan Province of China (Thun 2001: 15):

> being able to handle electronic orders from buyers, effectively forecast, plan, track production, and manufacture apparel quickly and flexibly, are skills that provide a far more enduring form of comparative advantage for Taiwanese firms than constantly scouring the globe for the lowest cost labor.

A study of European retailing (focusing on the United Kingdom, France and Scandinavia) found that Scandinavian retailers tended to concentrate their purchases among a relatively small number of foreign suppliers, while French retail sourcing was more dispersed. The study identified three different models of supply base management (Palpacuer, Gibbon and Thomsen 2003):

- A rules-based *United Kingdom model* emphasizing rationalization of the supply chain through formal supply chain management doctrines, with specialized functions centralized at corporate headquarters.
- A market-based *Scandinavian model* emphasizing concentrated sourcing networks, achieved by establishing strong personal relations with overseas manufacturers.
- A socially embedded *French model* emphasizing more open, informal and dispersed sourcing networks.

The growing size and dominance of larger EU and US retailers suggest important dynamics in the world economy: the experiences of Hong Kong (China), Singapore, Taiwan Province of China and the Republic of Korea – newly industrializing economies that relied on apparel and textile production as integral parts of successful development strategies – may prove difficult to replicate in a world where the retail end is more tightly controlled than it was 20 or 30 years ago.[9] Only countries with sizeable internal markets, such as China and India, may prove capable of moving up the apparel chain into higher-value-added activities, insofar as they are able to capitalize on their internal markets in developing indigenous retail capabilities.

B. The emergence of TNC producers in apparel and textiles

Although the global value chains in textiles and clothing are primarily buyer-driven, FDI plays an important role at the production stage. In many developing countries, foreign affiliates dominate such exports, and some producers have emerged as major transnational players, controlling production plants in several countries.

During the period 2002–2004, a total of 275 FDI projects related to the manufacturing of textiles and clothing were recorded.[10] As Table 6 shows, 38% of these projects were in developing Asia. The leading destinations in this region were China (with 48 projects), India (9), Viet Nam (8) and Thailand (8). The CEE countries accounted for another 29%, with Bulgaria (18), Hungary (13) and Poland (7) as the main targets (Table 7). Latin America and the Caribbean and Africa attracted 13% and 6% of all projects, respectively.

Table 6. FDI projects in textiles and clothing manufacturing, 2002–2004, by host region
(Number of projects; per cent)

Destination region	No. of projects	Share of total
Developing Asia-Pacific	106	38.5 %
Central and Eastern Europe	80	29.1 %
Latin America and the Caribbean	36	13.1 %
North America	20	7.3 %
Africa	16	5.8 %
Western Europe	14	5.1 %
Developed Asia-Pacific	3	1.0 %
Total	*275*	*100.0%*

Source: UNCTAD, based on LOCOmonitor.

Table 7. FDI projects in textiles and clothing manufacturing, 2002–2004, by host economy
(Number of projects)

Host economy	No. of projects
China	48
Bulgaria	18
United States	16
Hungary	13
Brazil	12
Viet Nam	8
India	9
Thailand	8
France	8
Poland	7
Uzbekistan	7
Morocco	6
Slovakia	6
Mexico	6
Croatia	6
Russian Federation	6
Other host economies	97
Total	275

Source: UNCTAD, based on LOCOmonitor.

While most (45%) of these projects originated in the European Union, almost 35% of them had an Asia-Pacific economy as their source (Table 8). In terms of number of FDI projects, the main Asian home economies were Japan (31 projects), Taiwan Province of China (15), Turkey (13), the Republic of Korea (11), Malaysia (7) and China (6). Thus, in many cases, TNC producers originate in the South, notably in East Asia. This aspect of the globalization of these industries has not received much attention to date, and only limited data are available. According to LOCOmonitor, among the top 10 most active foreign investors in textiles and clothing manufacturing during 2002–2004 were Hyosung (Republic of Korea), Hytex Integrated (Malaysia) and Zorlu Holdings (Turkey) (Table 9).

Table 8. FDI projects in textiles and clothing manufacturing, 2002–2004, by source region
(Number of projects; per cent)

Source region	No. of projects	Share of total
Western Europe	123	44.7 %
Asia-Pacific	95	34.6 %
North America	49	17.8 %
Africa and the Middle East	5	1.8 %
Latin America and the Caribbean	2	0.7 %
Central and Eastern Europe	1	0.4 %
Total	*275*	*100.0%*

Source: UNCTAD, based on LOCOmonitor.

Table 9. Top 10 investors in FDI projects in textiles and clothing manufacturing, 2002–2004
(Number of projects)

Company	Home economy	Number of projects
Toray Industries	Japan	11
DuPont	United States	5
Calzedonia	Italy	4
Fast Retailing	Japan	4
Gildan Activewear	Canada	4
Hyosung	Republic of Korea	4
Benetton	Italy	3
Hytex Integrated	Malaysia	3
Nena Models	Ireland	3
Zorlu Holdings	Turkey	3

Source: UNCTAD, based on information from LOCOmonitor.

Large retailers characteristically have large volume requirements, which lead them to consider only large producers (1,000+ workers) as potential suppliers. The elimination of quotas should facilitate a further geographical concentration of production and favour the growth of already strong TNC producers, not least those from Asia. Some of these firms already operate large factories under contract with large retailers and manufacturers.

Take the example of Top Form, the world's number one producer of brassieres. Based in Hong Kong (China), the company has more than 8,500 employees and production plants in China, Thailand and the Philippines. Thanks to its production scale, Top Form is the only brassiere maker to supply both Sara Lee and Vanity Fair (the two largest bra/undergarment companies in the United States). Its closest competitors, Acestyle and Clover, are privately owned makers also based in Hong Kong (China), but with a production capacity only about half that of Top Form's. To cope with increased demand, Top Form has been expanding its production facilities in China, most recently in Jiangxi, where labour costs are considerably lower than in Guangzhou or Shenzhen.[11]

The Esquel Group (Hong Kong (China)) is another example of a clothing sector TNC producer (Gibbon 2003b: 1823). It was founded in 1978 as a business selling sewing machines into China and receiving payment in made-up garments. Esquel claims to be the largest single cotton shirt manufacturer worldwide. At the turn of the century, its turnover was around $500 million; its stated employment globally in 2003 was 47,000. The company has textile production in China (where it is integrated backward as far as in-house cotton production) and apparel manufacturing in China, Malaysia, Mauritius, Sri

Lanka and Viet Nam. Previously, Esquel also manufactured in the Philippines and Jamaica (Gibbon 2003a). According to the company's website, the company manufactures for, among others, Tommy Hilfiger, Hugo Boss, Brooks Brothers, Abercrombie & Fitch, Nike, Lands' End and Muji, and major retailers such as Marks & Spencer, Nordstrom and Jusco.

Another example of TNC producers is Nien Hsing (Taiwan Province of China), the world's biggest jeans manufacturer, with production plants in Lesotho, Mexico, Nicaragua and Swaziland, employing some 17,000 workers (2001) and reporting nearly $300 million in revenues. Nien Hsing made 2% to 3% of all jeans consumed in the United States (Gibbon 2003a, 2003b), and in 2000 its Central American factories produced 40 million pairs of jeans for Wal-Mart, J. C. Penney, Kmart, the Gap, Sears and Target. China Garment Manufacturers (CGM) (Taiwan Province of China) is another denim maker, with apparel plants in Lesotho, Nicaragua and South Africa, and has also engaged in upstream textile integration in South Africa through the purchase of De Nim Textiles in KwaZulu-Natal (Gibbon 2003a, 2003b). Yupoong (Republic of Korea) is one of the world's largest cap makers, with manufacturing sites in Bangladesh, the Dominican Republic and Viet Nam. Boolim (Republic of Korea), a maker of athletic, casual and knit wear, is established in more than 25 countries. Carry Wealth Group (Taiwan Province of China), a producer of knit tops, woven bottoms and sweater tops, has plants in China, El Salvador, Indonesia, Lesotho and Viet Nam, and employed 8,500 workers globally in 2001 (Gibbon 2003a, 2003b).

An example from the footwear industry is also illustrative of the emergence of TNC producers. Yue Yuen/Pou Chen Industrial Holdings, which is based in Hong Kong (China), is the world's largest manufacturer of branded athletic and casual footwear, with nearly 160 million pairs of shoes produced in 2003.[12] It employs 242,000 people worldwide – almost as many as such well-known TNCs as Toyota, Nestlé or Unilever (UNCTAD 2004c) – which represents growth of 57% in only four years.[13] This includes an estimated 40,000 workers in its Dongguan (China) factory and 65,000 in its Huyen Binh Chanh factory in Viet Nam, reportedly the world's largest shoe factory complex. About 60% of Yue Yuen's footwear production is for Nike, Reebok and Adidas (Merk 2003); other clients include Polo Ralph Lauren, Kenneth Cole, Calvin Klein and NBA Properties.

Only a small number of case studies have documented the role of FDI in apparel and textiles. No systematic evidence is available to permit cross-country comparisons of how the leading producers are allocating their investments by country and region, or how FDI by specific producers will be impacted by the quota phase-out. Still, it is clear that in some developing countries the role of foreign producers is critical (see also the Annex). In Africa, recent increases in production from Lesotho, Madagascar, Mauritius and South Africa for the US market have mainly been accounted for by specialized assemblers and finishers of long runs of basic garments firms with their origin in East Asia (Gibbon 2003a). In Lesotho, the apparel industry is dominated by producers based in Taiwan Province of China; in South Africa, larger firms from Hong Kong (China) and Taiwan Province of China are the main exporters; Mauritian-owned firms account for the largest share of Madagascar's exports of textiles and clothing; whereas investments from Qatar and Sri Lanka have been important in Kenya's garment industry. Similarly, in Tunisia, about 45% of all employment in textiles and clothing is in foreign-owned enterprises.

The African Growth and Opportunity Act (AGOA) facilitated FDI to selected African economies, such as Kenya, Lesotho and Mauritius.[14] Since it has provided an effective 17% price advantage along with quota costs to all participating sub-Saharan African countries,[15] along with liberal rules of origin for least developed beneficiary countries (LDBC), it has had a significant impact on FDI and on apparel exports. US imports from Kenya, Lesotho, Madagascar, Mauritius and South Africa increased by 66% between 1999 (pre-AGOA) and 2001, to the point where they accounted for more than 90% of total African apparel exports. By way of comparison, imports to the EU from the five countries increased only 6% between 1999 and 2001. Growth reached 85% between 1999 and 2002, the most recent year for which data are available. Most of the growth in US imports was from Lesotho and Kenya (Gibbon 2003a).

FDI is also important in Latin America and the Caribbean. In the Dominican Republic, foreign producers (especially from the United States) dominate the export production undertaken in the country's export processing zones (EPZs), followed by domestic producers as well as foreign investors from the Republic of Korea, Panama, the Netherlands and Taiwan Province of China; in Honduras, only 17% of all apparel workers were employed in Honduran-owned factories in 2003; and in Mexico the most competitive producers are predominantly foreign-owned.

The picture is slightly different in Asia, where the role of foreign producers varies more by country. In Bangladesh, for example, 95% of the country's garment factories are locally owned, while in Cambodia foreign producers are relatively important. In 2001, the Cambodian Garment Manufacturers Association boasted more than 200 members, most of which were from Taiwan Province of China, China and the Republic of Korea.[16] In the case of China, foreign-invested enterprises accounted for 34.4% of the country's exports of textiles and clothing.[17] Much of the outward FDI in textiles and clothing comes from this part of the world.

To the extent that large contractors crowd out smaller competitors, concentration of production in a handful of companies and reduced competition at the factory level may counterbalance gains from economies of scale, thus possibly contributing to an increase in prices.

Increased concentration of production may in some cases facilitate worker organization, since larger factories are more sensitive to pressure from retailers and other buyers. A number of successful unionization drives has occurred in such factories in recent years, including the Kukdong (now Mexmode) apparel factory in Mexico, the BJ&B hat factory in the Dominican Republic (owned by Yupoon), and Hien Hsing factories in Mexico (Chentex) and Lesotho. In these examples, pressure on the factories and their clients (which included Nike, Reebok, the Gap, and other major US companies) by local independent labour unions, supported by US and EU unions and non-governmental organizations (NGOs), have caused parent companies to allow the formation of independent unions.[18]

More research is needed to establish when major retailers source directly from individual suppliers in a developing country, and when they rely on intermediaries. There is little evidence on what criteria determine this decision, or for what kind of products one or the other approach is preferred.

IV. Trade arrangements affecting the location of textiles and clothing production

A. The Multifibre Arrangement

The MFA, which entered into force in 1974, provided for bilateral agreements between trading nations that would regulate trade in apparel and textiles and allow for the imposition of import limits in the case of market disruption. As with previous restrictions in the area of textiles and clothing, it was supposed to be a temporary measure. The principal vehicle was an elaborate quota system whereby each country established import quotas for detailed categories of goods from each major trading partner (for example, specifying the number of women's wool sweaters the United States could import from Hong Kong (China) in a given year).

By 1981, 80% of all imports of apparel and textiles to the United States were covered by bilateral quota agreements and consultative mechanisms (Krishna and Tan 1997). The MFA was renegotiated four times until 1991, and then expired in 1994. The renegotiated versions of the MFA grew increasingly restrictive, as global textile and apparel trade expanded. As a general rule, quotas had to grow a minimum of 6% per year. However, this limit was often much lower owing to bilateral commitments that countries undertook on top of MFA obligations. Bilateral negotiations took place quite frequently, even on an annual basis, resulting in different quota annual growth rates for different products and countries.

MFA quotas were applied differently to different products and exporting countries. Some products and countries have been highly constrained by quotas, which greatly restricted the quantity of specific categories of apparel that could be exported. Other countries – or, more accurately, product lines within countries – were largely unaffected. The quota system has thus had several effects.

Quotas added to the cost of production, both indirectly, by restricting supply and thereby raising prices for consumers, and directly, since quotas were frequently sold and thus became a cost of doing business.[19] The imposition of quotas resulted in rents – the profit resulting from the difference in price that resulted from the quota. This rent was typically captured by the exporters who were allocated the quota. When quotas were sold, the rents accrued to whoever has the right to sell quota – in some cases the government of the exporting country, in others the exporters themselves. Relative to unrestricted goods, quotas caused the quantity of quota-restricted goods to decrease, and their price to increase (Tanzer 2000; Kathuria, Martin and Bhardwaj 2001). The actual impact on the indirect and direct costs of quotas to consumers remains a matter of some dispute, however.

As exporting countries have reached their quotas on specific products, production has shifted to less restricted countries and product categories. As a result, the quota system provided some developing countries with access to markets they would otherwise likely not have achieved.

Quota restrictions have affected industrial upgrading. In some quota-restricted countries (most notably in East Asia), they encouraged countries to move up into higher-value-added production – either of more costly products that were less quota-constrained, or into higher-value-added activities (such as design and marketing) in the apparel commodity chain, relocating low-cost production to less quota-constrained economies. Since the size of quotas was volume-based, moving into higher-value products was the only way for quota-constrained exporters to increase earnings from a given volume. Hong Kong (China), Taiwan Province of China and, more recently, China are examples (Tyagi 2003). Foreign producers in Mexico have also moved towards more integrated production, upgrading skills, investing in higher-value-added activities, and developing some quick response capabilities (Juststyle.com 2003a; Gereffi, Spener and Bair 2002). In other cases, to the extent that quotas have led to a relocation of production to relatively unconstrained developing countries, they may have provided a degree of protection that has reduced the incentive to adopt new technologies and upgrade.

Finally, quotas helped to protect jobs in high-cost countries. Indeed, this was their original purpose. Viet Nam's Trade Minister, citing IMF estimates, has reported that as many as 19 million jobs in developing countries may have been lost because of quota restrictions under the MFA. This figure rises to 27 million jobs when tariffs are included; a single job retained in developed countries is estimated to have caused the loss of 35 jobs in developing countries (Truong 2003; Chandrasekhar 2003). The IMF has estimated the export revenue loss to developing countries owing to trade restrictions at $40 billion, with $22 billion resulting from quotas alone (Chandrasekhar 2003).

B. The Agreement on Textiles and Clothing

The Agreement on Textiles and Clothing (ATC),[20] which was negotiated during the Uruguay Round, replaced the MFA regime and mandated the phase-out of quotas[21] on apparel and textiles over a 10-year period, beginning in January 1995. The phase-out was to occur over four phases until 2005. Two mechanisms have been employed to eliminate quotas: the phased removal of existing quotas, and accelerated growth rates for those remaining (Table 10).

Stages I and II (beginning 1 January 1995 and ending 31 December 2001) stipulated the elimination of quotas on no less than one-third of the importing country's textile and apparel import volume (based on 1990 levels). These initial changes had little impact, since unrestricted products were integrated. The final two phases had a bigger impact, since they applied to products more strongly constrained by the use of quotas.[22] Phase III, which began on 1 January 2002 and was completed on 31 December 2004, required the elimination of an additional 18% of quotas. The remaining 49% were eliminated on 1 January 2005. In fact, since the importing countries have a great deal of discretion over which quotas to eliminate, removal on the most restrictive categories was deferred until the very end.

The agreement also required an increase in those quotas that remained until the complete phase-out in 2005, with somewhat larger increases permitted for smaller supplying countries, at least initially.

The ATC itself ceased to exist on 1 January 2005; it was, in the words of the WTO (2004a), "the only WTO agreement that has self-destruction built in".[23]

Table 10. Stages of integration of textiles and apparel into GATT under ATC, 1995–2005
(Per cent)

Stage	Component 1 Share of importing country's textile and apparel trade to be free of quota (% of 1990 import volume)	Component 2 Growth rates in remaining quotas	
		Major supplying countries	Small supplying countries
1995–1997	16	16	25
1998–2001	17	25	27
2002–2004	18	27	27
2005	49	No quotas	No quotas

Source: Nathan Associates 2002.

Production locations have been unequally constrained by quotas. Economies that were once among the world's leading apparel exporters (Hong Kong (China), Taiwan Province of China, the Republic of Korea) have moved into higher-value-added activities than apparel production, and frequently had unfulfilled quotas in some categories of apparel. At the same time, countries such as China, India and Pakistan – which have experienced rapid growth in apparel exports – became more constrained over time (Diao and Somwaru 2001: 13). As is shown in Table 11, slightly more than half (53%) of apparel exports in 2001 from Asia to the United States were constrained by quotas, including nearly three fifths (59%) of China's exports.[24] At the other extreme, only 14% of Caribbean Basin Initiative (CBI) country exports, 13% of sub-Saharan AGOA member exports, and 0.5% of NAFTA member exports to the United States were constrained.

Table 11. Regional differences in quota constraints of US apparel imports, 2001
(Percentage)

Item	NAFTA	Sub-Saharan Africa (AGOA)	CBI	Asia	China
Unconstrained	99.5	87	86	47	41
Constrained	.5	13	14	53	59
Total	100.0	100	100	100	100

Source: Nathan Associates 2002, Figure 4.

C. Quotas and tariffs in preferential trade agreements

Many factors influence importers' decisions on where to source, and producers' decisions on where to invest. In assessing the impact of quota elimination, other trade agreements also need to be considered. The United States and the EU have preferential bilateral and regional trading agreements. Such agreements typically have rules of origin exempting apparel that uses the importing country's yarn, fabrics and dyeing from quota and tariff restrictions. Preferential access to the US and European markets has affected the efforts of selected developing countries to improve their competitive position (EU 2003a). The removal of quotas means the elimination of a key barrier to trade and may make tariff preferences relatively more important. The post–Uruguay Round tariff rates for 52% of imports of textiles and clothing in the United States range from 16% to 35%; and 54% of imports into the EU have rates of 10% to 15%. Some 55% of all Japanese imports of textiles and clothing face duties of 5% to 10% (UNCTAD 2004a). Consequently, preferential tariff treatment can still significantly affect the decision on where to locate production for exports.

Preferential trade agreements for the United States include the following:

- **The North American Free Trade Agreement (NAFTA)** effectively eliminates quota constraints and tariffs on apparel and textile trade with Mexico, provided that the apparel is made from North American fabrics and yarns. But NAFTA has built in some flexibility. For example, the agreement provides a *de minimis* rule which implies that a textile good containing non-originating fibres or yarns can qualify for full NAFTA benefits if the foreign content is 7% or less by weight of the component that determines the tariff classification. Moreover, apparel cut and sewn in one or more of the NAFTA countries from certain imported fabrics, which the parties agree are in short supply in North America, can qualify for preferential tariff treatment.
- **The African Growth and Opportunity Act (AGOA)** is part of the United States Trade and Development Act of 2000 and exempts from quota and tariffs imports from 38 African countries that meet certain requirements;[25] these include 23 countries that are eligible for preferential treatment in textiles and clothing. Only Zimbabwe, among major African apparel-exporting countries, is excluded.[26] In July 2004, AGOA was extended to 2015, and the special "third-country fabric" rule was extended until 30 September 2007.

- **The Caribbean Basin Trade Partnership Act (CBTPA) of 2000** is an expansion of the Caribbean Basin Initiative (CBI) and provides that certain apparel products may be imported into the United States duty- and quota-free. To qualify, products must be made with US fabrics wholly formed with US (unlike NAFTA, which requires only that products be made with yarns produced in any NAFTA signatory, i.e. Mexico, Canada or the United States). Currently, fewer than 15% of Caribbean exports are constrained by quota. This agreement is effective until September 2008. The proposed Central American Free Trade Agreement (CAFTA), if ratified,[27] will supersede and repeal the CBTPA (Hornbeck 2004). CAFTA includes the same "yarn forward" provisions as NAFTA (i.e. yarn can be produced in any signatory country, rather than only in the United States). In fact, since Central American countries lack their own yarn-producing industries, they will still have to import yarn from the United States for the foreseeable future (Bair and Dussel Peters 2004).

- **The Andean Trade Preferences Act (ATPA)[28]** is a 12-year-old agreement that lowers or eliminates duties on imports from Bolivia, Colombia, Ecuador and Peru by providing for duty- and quota-free imports of apparel made from US fabrics (as well as some specialized fabrics such as alpaca and llama) and products that use regional or US yarns, subject to certain caps. Some apparel items, such as footwear and apparel made of leather, can be included as long as they are not determined to be "import sensitive" with respect to other Andean country imports

(IMRA 2003; United States Office of the Trade Representative 2003).

For Asian LDCs, the United States does not provide preferential access beyond its Generalized System of Preferences, but the provisions for textiles and clothing are relatively modest in this scheme (UNCTAD 2004b: 232). Hence, most textiles and clothing exports from these Asian LDCs are subject to most-favoured-nation (MFN) rates.

The EU has expanded free trade agreements to the point where it "now trades duty- and quota-free with more than 30 countries in Central and Eastern Europe, Africa, Latin America and Asia" (Bora, Cernat and Turrini 2002: 17). Its preferential trade agreements include:

- **The Euro-Mediterranean Association Agreements** between the EU and 12 Mediterranean "partners,"[29] which establishes a free trade area to be fully implemented by 2010.

- **The EU–African, Caribbean and Pacific (ACP) Agreement,** which allows most ACP exports (including 80% of all industrial products) to enter the EU quota- and duty-free.

- **The Everything but Arms (EBA) initiative**, announced in September 2000, which eliminates quotas and tariffs on all imports into the EU from the LDCs, with the exception of arms and munitions. The EU is contemplating modifications of the rules of origin for LDCs.[30]

D. Factors mitigating the effects of quota removal

The elimination of quotas does not, by itself, imply a fully competitive global market for textile and apparel production, for several reasons:

- **Regional trading blocks may become more important.** The relaxing of quota constraints increases the relative importance

of geographical proximity (which reduces delivery time), contributing to the strength of trading blocs such as NAFTA, an expanded EU and ASEAN (see discussions in Tyagi 2003; Juststyle.com 2003a; O'Rourke 2000; Kahn 2003; Ricupero 2003; Truong 2003).[31]

- **Tariff barriers will remain and possibly increase in importance even after quotas are eliminated.** While the quota exemptions are no longer relevant post-ATC, favourable tariff treatment continues to play a role. Tariffs vary considerably across countries.

- **Anti-dumping measures.** Domestic textile and apparel lobbies in the United States and the EU are likely to argue that significant price reductions are the result of dumping, calling for "trade remedy actions" such as dumping investigations. Anti-dumping measures will doubtless continue to be invoked by importing countries as a way to protect domestic industries from low-cost imports.[32] Between 1993 and 1998, the volume of cotton fabric imports into the EU was reduced from 59% to 38% for Egypt, India, Indonesia and Pakistan, all of which were involved in anti-dumping investigations. Such investigations are not likely to diminish after quotas are removed (ITCB 2003; Chandrasekhar 2003).

- **Safeguards against "market disruptions".** Article 6 of the ATC recognizes the need for a "transitional safeguard" during the phase-out period. (This protection, along with the ATC itself, came to an end 1 January 2005.) Under this provision of the ATC, transitional safeguard action could be taken by a WTO member when it was demonstrated that "a particular product [was] being imported into its territory in such increased quantities as to cause serious damage, or actual threat thereof, to the domestic industry producing like and/or directly competitive products". In the first two stages of the liberalization, a large number of requests for consultations regarding safeguard measures were made, but it appears that recourse to safeguards was subsequently declined (Nordås 2004; WTO 2001). The WTO Agreement on Safeguards contains provisions permitting a member country to restrict imports temporarily "if its domestic industry is injured or threatened with injury caused by a surge in imports". This safeguard provision includes criteria for determining whether or not the injury is sufficiently serious to warrant protections; specifies conditions for the protections; and requires that they be progressively liberalized as long as they are in force.[33]

V. The impact of quota elimination

The immediate beneficiaries of quota elimination have been predicted to be consumers, who should experience declining costs of textile and apparel products as production shifts to the lowest-cost countries and quota rents are eliminated (Slater 2003) – although the size of this benefit remains subject to much debate. Textile and apparel workers in the high-cost countries, as well as less competitive developing countries, have been predicted to be disadvantaged by the phase-out. Econometric simulations of the aggregate global benefits of trade liberalization of all sorts vary enormously, from a low of $6 billion to a high of $324 billion, depending on the underlying assumptions. The contribution of ATC reform has been estimated to range from two thirds of all gains to a mere 5% (EU 2003a; Walkenhorst 2003). Clearly, this is not an exact science.

In terms of the resulting international production structure, the quota elimination is likely to lead to consolidation into even larger companies and a smaller number of supplying countries, mainly to leverage achievable economies of scale (Speer 2002). Industry sources claim that large retailers and manufacturers such as the Gap, J. C. Penney, Liz Claiborne and Wal-Mart that once sourced from 50 or more countries now source from 30–40. Without quotas, it is predicted that the number will fall to 10–15 (Juststyle.com 2003a; Malone 2002; McGrath 2003). So competition among garment-producing countries should increase, contributing to more pressure to reduce production costs, and therefore to lower wages. This may also mean increased risk for weaker labour standards (Maquila Solidarity Network 2002–2003). At the same time, as is noted above, concentration of production into larger factory units may in some cases help facilitate worker organization.

At the same time, numerous factors other than quotas shape the decisions on where to locate apparel and textile production, including labour costs, quality, productivity, time to market, reliability, and the presence of synergistic forces in apparel-producing industrial districts. Another factor is the ability of a country's producers to engage in full-package production – that is, to go beyond simple assembly and supply the client with a finished product by providing designing, sourcing, cutting, sewing, assembling, labelling, packaging and shipping. In one study of the CEOs of 14 major textile and apparel producers or trading companies in Hong Kong (China), conducted in 2000 and replicated in 2003, respondents indicated the relative importance of 18 factors in shaping their sourcing decisions. The top-ranked six items, in descending order of importance, were (1) politics and stability, (2) the quality of transportation infrastructure, (3) the quality of telecommunications infrastructure, (4) local policies affecting trade and development, (5) labour costs and (6) policies affecting labour (such as health and working environment) (Spinanger and Verma 2003; Andriamananjara, Dean and Spinanger 2004). Significantly, labour costs ranked fifth. Quotas did not make the top six determinants in the 2003 survey, although they ranked second in the 2000 survey.[34]

There is broad apprehension that the elimination of textile and apparel quotas will immediately benefit a select number of developing countries as production and export bases – notably those that possess a strong and diversified mix of textile and apparel products; engage in full-package production; produce high-quality, high-value-added products; and service diverse markets outside the United States and the EU.[35]

A recent review of various studies found that the largest benefits are most likely to accrue primarily to China and India (WWD 2003a; see also Truong 2003). Pakistan, Viet Nam, the Republic of Korea, Hong Kong (China) and Taiwan Province of China. Some locations with preferential access to the US and EU markets will also likely remain attractive locations (Moore 2003; Jones 2003). It is also possible that major suppliers that have developed strong commercial ties with the United States will continue as major suppliers after quota elimination (Jones 2003).

Many developing countries are expected to decline in attractiveness as less competitive locations for export-oriented FDI, at least in the short term.[36] LDCs and small exporters that have enjoyed quota- and duty-free treatment of their exports to the United States and the EU, and that rely heavily on exports of a limited range of assembled garments as well as compete on the basis of price rather than quality, are the most vulnerable to the expected heightened level of competition post-ATC (UNCTAD 2004a; Manjur 2002). As was noted above, several LDCs are among those with particularly high dependence on exports of textiles and clothing. In a quota-free environment, these exporters face increasingly intense competition. Countries in which more than three quarters of all apparel exports have been in highly constrained quota categories (and therefore will lose this advantage when quotas are eliminated) include Haiti and Lesotho among the LDCs, as well as El Salvador, Honduras, Jamaica, Kenya and Nicaragua (Hillman 2003). Many of these countries also have limited capabilities to adjust to the impacts of ATC expiry.

Spinanger and Verma (2003) used the Global Trade Analysis Project (GTAP) model to estimate the impact of the end of the ATC on textile and apparel exports from individual countries, as well as the larger impacts of the further trade liberalization that is slated to result from China's full accession to the WTO.[37] Their model estimates that quota elimination alone would result in a 6% increase in China's textile exports and an 88% increase in clothing exports. The corresponding gains for full trade liberalization are even larger (39% for textiles, 168% for apparel). Under their simulations, most countries would benefit in terms of textile exports post-ATC; the principal exceptions are Canada, the United States and Mexico; the EU; and Africa and the Middle East.[38] With regard to apparel exports, the only economies to benefit in their study were Hong Kong (China), China, Viet Nam, India, and the United States.[39] These results have been supported by surveys conducted with CEOs of 14 major textile and apparel companies and trading houses in Hong Kong (China) in 2000 and 2003, in which the respondents were asked about their future sourcing plans (Spinanger and Verma 2003; Andriamananjara, Dean and Spinanger 2004).

Nordås (2004) also used a GTAP model to estimate the impact of the end of the ATC. While her simulations suggests that China and India will gain further market shares in trade in textiles and clothing post-ATC, she also stresses that such simulations fail to take into account "recent developments in the organization of the textile and clothing sector" – for example, increased vertical specialization, which "implies that the inputs embodied in the final product cross borders several times and such trade is very sensitive to the tariff level" (p. 34). More importantly, perhaps, lean retailing makes time to market increasingly important, especially in the fashion clothing industry. Hence, "therefore, countries close to the major markets are likely to be less affected by competition from India and China than has been anticipated in previous studies. Mexico, the Caribbean, Eastern Europe and North Africa are therefore likely to remain important exporters to the US and EU respectively, and possibly maintain their market shares" (p. 34). It has also been noted that GTAP models suffer from an incomplete reflection of actual trade protection patterns. Moreover, they assume that resources released from one sector may flow to another without significant disruptions in the short or medium term (Mayer 2004).

It is thus important to caution against results emerging from studies using the GTAP model. While some recent modelling studies are valuable for evaluating the likely outcome of alternative scenarios, they must be carefully interpreted, as results depend crucially on the assumptions made in each model. As was noted in the introduction to this section, econometric modelling is not an exact science, and estimated impacts vary considerably between different studies (UNCTAD 2004a).

Quota elimination removed one advantage from those countries that currently benefit from preferential trade agreements. While such countries continue to benefit from preferential tariff treatment, tariffs are generally less costly to exporting countries than are quota restrictions.[40] The most exposed countries are those that lack preferential (tariff-free) access to the US market.

Mexico, for example, benefited from NAFTA between 1994 and 2000. But in a post-ATC world, NAFTA does not guarantee success: Mexico needs to develop full-package production capabilities. Currently US firms control design and marketing, while Mexican companies engage mainly in assembly. Moreover, Mexico's experience under NAFTA suggests some of the limitations of relying on apparel exports as a development strategy. Even during the height of the post-NAFTA production boom, only a small number of well-connected local firms benefited, with much production and assembly subcontracted out to small firms. The downturn and sluggish recovery in the US economy since 2000 have reversed the fortunes of even the largest Mexican exporters, and much apparel production in the past couple of years has shifted to lower-wage areas (notably in China). Only the more capital-intensive segments of the textile and apparel commodity chain (textile mills, modern laundries and computerized cutting rooms) seem relatively secure (Bair and Gereffi 2003).

At the regional level, aggregated risks resulting from quota elimination, at least in terms of US apparel imports, are estimated in Table 12. The highest risks are faced by NAFTA countries (in this case, Mexico), in which the preferential advantage was lost when quotas were eliminated, although they keep the advantage of tariff-free access. An estimated 90% of Mexico's apparel exports to the United States are at high risk, as are 75% of CBI exports to the United States. The sub-Saharan LDCs of AGOA face a similar situation, with 84% of their apparel exports to the United States at high risk (see the Annex for a more detailed discussion). The impact on Asian countries is lower, and only 5% of China's exports are perceived to be at high risk.

Table 12. US apparel imports, by source and risk level, 2002–2005
(Percentage)

Risk level	NAFTA	Sub-Saharan Africa (AGOA)	CBI	Asia	China
Low	9.3	2.2	11.2	16.4	44.0
Moderate	0.5	13.6	14.0	52.3	51.1
High	90.2	84.2	74.8	31.4	4.9
Total	100.0	100.0	100.0	100.0	100.0

Source: Nathan Associates 2002, Figure 5.

Note. "Low" risk implies that products are already not restrained by quotas (so quota elimination will make no difference). "Moderate" risk applies to products that are currently restrained for producers in the region, restraints that will end when quotas are eliminated. "High"-risk products are currently not restrained for producers in the given region but are restrained for producers in other regions; the competitive advantage arising from this situation will end with the elimination of quotas.

China is the world's largest (and, among major producers, most rapidly growing) exporter of apparel and deserves particular attention. China has long been set up for full-package production, making it relatively easy for US, European and Japanese companies to source reliably completed garments from Chinese factories. This, combined with the country's vast supply of productive low-cost labour, will accelerate the movement of apparel production to China.[41] One analysis of actual locational shifts in production that occurred during Stage II of the ATC (1998–2001) found that exports from China more than doubled in the first half of 2004 in a number of categories such as brassieres and infant wear.[42] The analysis further showed that:

"the market shares...of non-quota constrained suppliers – NAFTA and the CBI – dropped by an average of one-third between 1997 and 2001. Most ominous for other suppliers, between the first quarters of 2001 and 2002, China's market share increased 5 percentage points, while other suppliers' market share declined" (Nathan Associates 2002: 13).

China has been projected to benefit most from the complete phase-out. Its apparel exports had already reached $52 billion in 2003 (up from $41 billion in 2002), approximately 22% of the world total (Table 1). Some studies predict that China may account for as much as half of the world market after 2005 (Francois and Spinanger 2002). In addition, China's internal market for clothing has been predicted to double, from roughly $50 billion in 2000 to around $100 billion in 2010 (WWD 2003a). In the case of textiles, China's share of the world market stood around 15% in 2003, up from 6% in 1990 (Table 3). Recently released data from the Government of China indicate that total exports of textiles and clothing in 2004 increased to some $97 billion, more than 20% higher than in 2003.[43]

As was noted in Table 7, China was also the world's largest recipient of new FDI projects in textiles and clothing in 2002–2004. It is estimated that, out of China's overall exports of textiles and clothing, foreign-investment enterprises accounted for about one third in 2004.[44] Among the top 10 exporters of textiles and clothing from China in 2003, three were classified as foreign-invested enterprises, all of them registered in Hong Kong (Table 13).

Table 13. Largest exporters of textiles and clothing, China, 2003
(Million dollars)

Rank	Company	Exports ($ million)	Home economy
1	Guangdong Silk Corporation (Group)	1 171	China
2	China Worldbest Group Co. Ltd.	1 152	China
3	Youngor Group Co. Ltd.	521	China
4	Shandong Weiqiao Pioneering Group Co. Ltd.	432	China
5	Dongguan Fu'an Weaving, Printing and Dyeing Co. Ltd.	409	Hong Kong (China)
6	Zhejiang Yongtong Dyeing and Weaving Co. Ltd.	..	China
7	Veken Holding Group Co. Ltd.	352	China
8	Dongguan Deyongjia Weaving and Clothing Co. Ltd.	327	Hong Kong (China)
9	Nanshan Group	..	China
10	Dongguan Shatian Lihai Weaving, Printing and Dyeing Co. Ltd.	132	Hong Kong (China)

Source: UNCTAD, based on data from China National Textile Industry Council (CNTIC) and export data from MOFCOM.
Note: The ranking is based on available export data from MOFCOM and therefore differs slightly from the ranking according to CNTIC.

Official statistics from the Government of China confirm a strong interest among foreign companies in expanding in textiles and clothing in China. The number of foreign-invested enterprises in this industry increased in 2003 alone by 5,856 companies, bringing the total to almost 20,000 foreign-invested enterprises in textiles and clothing. That year the corresponding value of FDI inflows amounted to $5.3 billion, or 10% of the country's overall FDI inflows (China: MOFCOM 2004). The surge in such FDI suggests that many TNCs were expanding into China in anticipation of the removal of quotas at the end of 2004.

China's potential is based on several factors (Nathan Associates 2002; Speer 2002; USITC 2003; Moore 2003).

- First, "the breadth and variety of China's apparel production is unmatched anywhere in the world…no other country comes close to shipping as many [10-digit SIC] headings as China" (Moore 2003: 2).
- Second, the country is well endowed with the raw materials needed to supply its own textile industry. It has, for example, the world's largest production capacities for cotton, silk, and man-made fibres such as flax and ramie. (The principal exception is wool, which it gets mainly from Australia and New Zealand.) It also has ready access to high-quality imported fabrics.[45]
- Third, in recent years, China's fixed exchange rate against the dollar has made its exports increasingly

competitive as the dollar has depreciated against other currencies.

- Fourth, China's textile and apparel industries benefit from marketing, managerial and financial expertise from investors (from Hong Kong (China) and Taiwan Province of China). The country has a skilled labour force that is difficult to match elsewhere in the world, particularly when coupled with China's low hourly wages. Thus, it is well placed in terms of productivity, management skills and technology, low-wage labour, transportation costs, material costs and product quality.

China's success in the competitive Japanese and Australian markets suggests that it can supply high-quality apparel. In Australia, since quotas were abolished, virtually all apparel imports have been supplied from China. While other factors (such as geographical proximity) clearly play a role in Chinese exports to Japan and Australia, the absence of quotas is important. As Table 14 shows, Japanese companies also accounted for the highest number of new FDI projects in textiles and clothing manufacturing in China during 2002–2004, according to LOCOmonitor. Toray Industries, Sumitomo Group, Kaneka and Matsuoka are examples of Japanese TNCs that have expanded manufacturing in China.

Table 14. Number of FDI projects in textiles and clothing manufacturing in China, 2002–2004, by source economy

(Number of projects; per cent)

Source economy	No. of projects	Share of total
Japan	11	22.9 %
United States	8	16.7 %
Republic of Korea	6	12.5 %
Denmark	3	6.3 %
Greece	3	6.3 %
Malaysia	3	6.3 %
Taiwan Province of China	2	4.2 %
Turkey	2	4.2 %
Other home economies	10	20.8 %
Total	*48*	*100.0 %*

Source: UNCTAD, based on information from LOCOmonitor.

At the same time, other factors may limit the extent to which production will shift to China. The expected growth in China's exports may be mitigated by treaties that continue to provide preferential tariff treatments to selected trading partners, as well as by the advantages of geography for quick replenishment. Moreover, China's WTO accession agreement includes a "transitional product-specific safeguard mechanism", according to which

In cases where products of Chinese origin are being imported into the territory of any WTO Member in such increased quantities or under such conditions as to cause or threaten to cause market disruption to the domestic producers of like or directly competitive products, the WTO Member so affected may request consultations with

China with a view to seeking a mutually satisfactory solution, including whether the affected WTO Member should pursue application of a measure under the Agreement on Safeguards… If consultations do not lead to an agreement between China and the WTO Member concerned within 60 days of the receipt of a request for consultations, the WTO Member affected shall be free, in respect of such products, to withdraw concessions or otherwise to limit imports only to the extent necessary to prevent or remedy such market disruption.[46]

The accession agreement uses the concept of "market disruption", stipulates the procedures to be followed, places limitations on duration, and provides that the safeguard mechanism will come to an end 12 years after China's accession to the WTO. First, Chinese textiles and clothing exports will be subject to the special textiles safeguard provision until 31 December 2008, and the United States has already invoked the special safeguards provision in China's accession agreement. In December 2003, the United States implemented import quotas on China's exports of five categories, three of which had been liberalized in 2002 (Mayer 2004: 16). Second, from 2009 to 2013, WTO members can apply a standard WTO safeguard mechanism selectively targeting only China. Third, the application of the market economy principle to China in determining anti-dumping and countervailing measures is deferred for 15 years after the date of accession (until December 2016).

Some WTO members (Argentina, the European Communities, Hungary, Mexico, Poland, the Slovak Republic, Turkey) made reservations in annex 7 to China's accession agreement with the WTO to maintain prohibitions, quantitative restrictions and other measures against selected imports from China in a manner inconsistent with the WTO Agreement. In general, the WTO members committed to phasing out these restrictions by 2005 at the latest. Mexico will be permitted to keep anti-dumping practices in place until 2007.

Furthermore, in December 2004, the Government of China announced that it planned to introduce a minimum export tax on each garment, regardless of what they would cost. In effect, that would mean a relatively higher tax on low-cost than on high-cost items. In a statement, the Commerce Department indicated that the measure would be used to encourage the production of higher-end textiles and apparel instead of a full range.[47] Moreover, in order to monitor developments of exports in the post-quota environment, from 1 March 2005 the Interim Method for Automatic License of Textiles Export will be implemented. This means that an export license will be applied for 216 textile products, shirts, underwear, trousers and children's clothing.[48]

There is no universal agreement that most production will move to China. One business consulting firm warns against over-

estimating the ability of China to overwhelm other garment-exporting nations (Flanagan 2003). China does not offer the lowest prices and is disadvantaged in terms of turnaround time. There is also growing competition among retailers on lead time for as much as 30% of their total imports; this may favour sourcing closer to home – for example, from Turkey and Romania for the EU.[49] Retailers may also be reluctant to rely on only one source country and may, for reasons of risk diversification, retain existing supplier relations with producers in other countries. The same may apply to TNC producers. For example, Top Form, the largest brassieres maker in the world, indicated that it does not plan to abandon its production facilities in Thailand and Philippines post-ATC, mainly to avoid putting all its eggs in one basket.[50]

One study argues that the emergence of lean retailing during the 1990s made timeliness (defined as a "short and reliable lag between order and delivery") more important than before, thereby favouring suppliers that are close to major markets (Evans and Harrigan 2004: 11). Many apparel items are continuously reordered, requiring "rapid replenishment". Analyzing data provided by a US department store chain, the study estimates that "for high-replenishment products, proximity to the United States is equivalent to a 53 percentage point reduction in tariffs, while for goods with a replenishment percentage of 25% proximity is equivalent to a 20 percentage point tariff reduction" (p. 14). This may suggest that geographical advantage will remain important even when trade policy is liberalized.

This conclusion is not undisputed, however. It has been argued that, while a three-day shipping time from Mexico would seem to compare favourably with 12 days from Hong Kong (China) or 15 days from China, the overall advantage (Dee 2003: 1):

> lies in the ability of Hong Kong supply chain managers to cover the entire product chain, from design onwards, and to shepherd a product from sample making to delivery in just 3 weeks. In doing so, they may divide the production and sourcing process into as many as 10 or 12 stages across the whole Asian region,

reconfiguring its architecture for each new order. And with this extent of value added, they find it a small cost to air freight the final product.

The ability to engage in full-package production may neutralize Mexico's and the CBI economies' geographical proximity to the United States. Concerning the challenges facing countries in Central America and the Caribbean, a succinct summary was provided by ECLAC (2004: 90–92):

In general, the manufacturers operating in these economies are subsidiaries of foreign branded manufacturers (especially of women's undergarments) or domestic or foreign firms that compete for assembly contracts (particularly for men's wear) from large United States retailers. This is why the full-package concept has not flourished in the Central American and Caribbean countries, since their competitive advantages are derived strictly from the characteristics that make them

well-suited to final product assembly: EPZs, preferential access to the United States and low wages... The industry's future prospects – particularly in Honduras and the Dominican Republic, where it is still very important – are not very promising. ... [These countries] did not reach the level of industrial and technological upgrading needed to sustain exports, and some of these countries are caught in the low-value-added trap.

Finally, for some locations (notably Japan, the Republic of Korea, Taiwan Province of China, and possibly some other ASEAN locations), strong growth in China may result in increased imports of textiles and other inputs to its growing apparel export industry (Shafaeddin 2002). On the apparel side, China is a much smaller importer, although its imports have grown from virtually zero in 1990 to more than $1 billion. So far, various East Asian economies have accounted for the bulk of those imports, which constitute primarily high-fashion, high-quality clothing.

VI. Conclusions and policy options

Based on the above review of trade and investment patterns in textiles and clothing, this final section consolidates the main findings regarding the likely impact of the phasing out of quotas on the allocation of FDI and export-oriented production. The section also highlights some policy options, drawing on individual country cases reported in the Annex, with fairly broad applicability. Policies are divided into two categories – those related to action at the level of the textile and apparel industries, and those concerning country-level policies. This distinction is somewhat arbitrary, since changes at the industry level frequently require various forms of state support.

A. The impact of quota phase-out

This study has shown that large corporations play an increasingly important role in the allocation of export-oriented production of apparel and textiles. Global apparel production has been characterized by the growth of large retailers along with the emergence of large transnational producers. The location of apparel production is thus dictated by the sourcing and production strategies of a handful of players. The world's 40 largest retailers (mainly from the United States and the EU) possess the ability to direct FDI to any given location. Very large retailers tend to place very large orders, which leads them to seek out very large factories. Furthermore, the trend towards "lean retailing", mediated by data sharing and electronic interchange, has enabled retailers to bring their suppliers under more direct control. These changes, in turn, seem to favour producers especially from Hong Kong (China), Taiwan Province of China and the Republic of Korea. They have the know-how, technological capacity and flexibility to manage tightly dispersed production networks. Moreover, retailers and manufacturers often follow their suppliers, preferring to work with large transnational producers with whom they have done prior business, rather than with smaller, unfamiliar suppliers.

There are many factors beyond quotas that determine the location of textiles and clothing production, but most studies suggest that quota elimination will immediately benefit a handful of developing countries as production and export bases. Typical features of these locations are an ability to produce a diversified mix of textile and apparel products, the capacity to engage in full-package production, access to high-quality supplies at competitive costs, and the skills needed for higher-value-added products. China and India as well as a number of other Asian locations are particularly well positioned from this perspective. Remaining trade preferences will also affect the location of textiles and clothing production, however, as will the need for close market proximity for replenishment production. This will provide opportunities for countries in Africa, Latin America and the Caribbean as well as in CEE to develop their roles as export bases to the US and European markets. At the same time, tariff preferences tend to erode over time, and the importance of geographical proximity has to be assessed against the ability to manage the overall production and distribution process. Hence, over time, countries seeking a place among the preferred export locations will have to improve their competitiveness and capabilities.

Many African countries, including many LDCs, are expected to be adversely affected by the quota phase-out. Most African-based exporters do not yet have the economies of scale that will be required to compete effectively with more developed apparel industries. Existing and planned preferential trade agreements could further exacerbate Africa's problems. These include the United States–Central American Free Trade Agreement (CAFTA) and the Free Trade Area of the Americas (FTAA), if negotiated. Meanwhile, future reductions in the MFN tariff rates as a result of multilateral trade negotiations would reduce the benefit of having preferential market access.

For Latin American and Caribbean exporters, there is a need for upgrading to meet the new competitive situation. Mexico has been relatively unsuccessful in taking advantage of NAFTA to develop the kinds of full-package production capabilities that make production in Asia increasingly attractive, and it has recently lost export market shares. Meanwhile, although some Central American and CBI countries (such as the Dominican Republic, El Salvador, Guatemala and Honduras) have increased their share of US apparel imports in recent years, all suffer from an inability to provide the kind of full-package production that permitted East Asia to thrive in the past.

Among Asian countries, most studies have predicted that China and India will benefit from the phase-out of quotas, although the magnitude of these changes is hard to establish with any accuracy. Many countries in the region (but especially the smaller ones) have been highly dependent on the quota system. In South Asia, for example, garments are made mainly for buyer-driven mass merchandise and discount chains. Only India and Pakistan have raw materials such as cotton. Thus, the region currently competes almost exclusively on the basis of low labour costs, which means that the quota phase-out carries with it a risk of job losses, wage cuts and job quality deterioration.

B. How the emergence of large producers affects policy making

Whereas the global textiles and clothing industries have been presented as predominantly buyer-driven value chains, it is clear that FDI has come (and will continue) to play a key role in these industries. As is shown in the case studies included in the Annex, foreign producers (especially from Asia) dominate production in many developing countries. Future investment decisions may lead to a growing consolidation of both retailers and suppliers into a smaller number of larger firms, a process that may in fact provide a point of leverage for influencing investment. There have been a number of instances where NGOs (along with US government agencies) have pressured retailers into working with their suppliers to improve working conditions in factories in Mexico, the Caribbean and elsewhere. Perhaps investment decisions could be influenced by a similar strategy. Cambodia's participation in an ILO inspection programme, which secures preferential treatment for exports to the United States, is a relevant example. This programme has included preferential treatment in the form of extra quota (up to an additional 14%) and lower tariffs (see Annex).

The policy challenges for developing countries are twofold. First, these countries must become attractive for investors without competing on labour costs alone, since there will always be competition from other low-cost production sites. Some suggestions are offered below to help accomplish this task. Second, the countries must seek to attract investment under conditions that will enable them to move up from simple assembly to full-package production and eventually original brand manufacture (thereby replicating the successful developmental experience of the East Asian newly industrializing economies). This requires a partnership between indigenous suppliers and their customers in the United States and the EU. The emergence of large TNC producers makes such partnerships more difficult, however. Although there is hardly any research on the forward and backward linkages generated by the mainly East Asian suppliers that are becoming increasingly central actors in this industry, technology transfer – and industrial learning – in a host country is more likely to occur when the suppliers are local firms (UNCTAD 2001a).

C. National economic policies

A range of policy responses are needed at the national level of developing countries, as is noted in the Annex to this study. In many apparel-exporting countries, lengthy turnaround times handicap competitiveness, particularly in high-value-added production, where time to market is a key factor for more fashion-sensitive items. This underlines the importance of infrastructure improvements to support efficient trade logistics. Key areas for such improvements include public investments in dry ports and creation of EPZs, provision of incentives (grants, loans, tax relief) in line with international commitments to develop supportive industries, and removal of bottlenecks that result in delays in shipping and customs clearance. A concrete example is the introduction of electronic data interchange at ports and customs houses to facilitate faster clearance of imported fabrics. Since financial resources are obviously key to developing local industries, providing direct funding to build capacity in the export sector can be important, as well as incentives that reduce freight charges and utility costs, or the removal of export duties and other taxes. In countries where the tax system is biased against particular inputs (e.g. man-made fibres in India, which are subject to special taxes, industrial licensing requirements and import duties), changes in the tax code may be necessary.

Labour law reform is another largely untapped area for change, but one that has not been seriously addressed in studies reviewed for this volume. A growing number of leading retailers and manufacturers in the United States and the EU are concerned about harsh labour practices (and the adverse publicity that can result from exposure of such practices). In fact, many cases of extremely poor working conditions have been reported in various studies of textiles and clothing factories in some developing countries, and there has been concern that conditions would deteriorate further post-ATC, owing to intensified competition (UNCTAD 2004a). In response, major retailers have developed private codes of conduct that require basic labour rights and protections in their contracted factories. In the United States, two NGOs – the Fair Labor Association and the Worker Rights Consortium – have been created to oversee the implementation of such codes.[51] The codes typically call for adequate wage and hour protection, job security, prohibition against pregnancy testing (and against firing female workers who become pregnant), health and safety guarantees, and the right to form independent labour unions to engage in

collective bargaining. Countries with labour laws consistent with these codes of conduct – and the means to enforce them – could effectively market themselves to the socially more conscious US and EU retailers and manufacturers. At the same time, further analysis is needed to assess how such private codes may affect the ability of developing-country firms to compete internationally. The risk of such codes' being used to protect developed-country markets from imports post-ATC deserves scrutiny (UNCTAD 2004a).

Several recommendations presented in the case studies call for bilateral government agreements with importing countries that would favour local industries. These range from encouraging developed countries to provide companies with technical assistance to enable them better to absorb workers displaced by quota phase-out (Sri Lanka) to retaining or securing preferential trade treatment with the United States and the EU (for example, under the General System of Preferences).

Finally, the development of regional trading blocs is a strategy sometimes mentioned. For example, the Honduran Ambassador to the United States has called for the integration of NAFTA with Central America, the rest of the Caribbean Basin region, and eventually the Andean region. In his view, the Central American Free Trade Agreement (CAFTA), awaiting ratification, should reduce complexities in customs and sourcing regulations, as well as simplify the rules of origin. Moreover, preferential benefits under regional trade agreements should not be limited to imported fabrics from the importing country. For example, the requirement that benefits under the AGOA be restricted to apparel made from US or sub-Saharan yarns and fabrics is predicted to lower African apparel exports by as much as a third once quotas are eliminated. A delay in the implementation of such restrictions could help countries that are struggling to develop competitive apparel industries in a post-quota world. The recent extension of the LDBC provision can be seen as a step in that direction.

D. Industry-level policies

National policy making can be complemented by various industry-level efforts to increase the competitiveness of local production. Those developing countries most exposed to risks associated with the quota phase-out tend to suffer from a common set of interlocking problems at the level of production. Their industries are typically characterized by low levels of efficiency, productivity and quality. They often rely exclusively on a single market (the United States or the EU) and specialize in a handful of product lines rather than providing product diversity. Backward linkages to indigenous textile industries as well as forward linkages to markets are typically absent, and most producers are engaged in simple assembly work at the bottom of the value chain. To stay competitive, countries need to develop the capability to respond quickly to frequent changes in the market place.

Enhancing work productivity through skills training and technological upgrading is a key step towards diversifying production into higher-value-added garments such as the more fashion-sensitive women's wear categories. As is highlighted in the Annex, various initiatives have already been taken by some countries to address this challenge. In Sri Lanka, for example, the Government has levied a garment tax to fund technological upgrading and skills enhancement in the industry. The Commercial Minister of Sri Lanka has called for the introduction of design and product development professional courses for industry participants in the country's universities. In Bangladesh, Nari Uddug Kendra – the Centre for Women's Initiatives – has conducted a study of worker retraining needs.

The industry has also been called on to invest in information technology in order to reduce lead times, as well as to develop professional marketers who can more effectively promote the country's textile and apparel products. The creation of national business associations in key export markets is seen as one way of helping to secure strong business contacts.

Developing indigenous sources of textiles, accessories and other inputs is another step that is frequently recommended. Pakistan's Textile Vision 2005, for example, calls for increasing output of apparel made of synthetics by encouraging the production of polyesters and other man-made fibres, so that the industry is not overly reliant on cotton fibres. Of course, improving backward linkages presupposes the capacity to develop an indigenous textile industry. One specific recommendation, made for the Nepalese industry but applicable to other countries, is to develop products for emerging market niches. Such niches could include socially and environmentally conscious consumers. This would focus on the manufacture and sale of eco-friendly fabrics, as well as garments aimed at consumers who are concerned with working conditions. There is potentially a large market for such products – initially in Europe, where consumer awareness already exists, but also in the United States, where a growing anti-sweatshop movement has led major branded labels such as Gap Inc. and Nike to be far more cognizant of labour practices in their contracted factories (Bonacich and Appelbaum 2000; Featherstone 2002; Appelbaum 2000, forthcoming; Esbenshade 2004).

Annex:
Case Studies

Limited evidence is available on the role of FDI in textiles and clothing production in developing countries. For the present publication, some 60 studies and reports from a wide range of organizations were reviewed to ascertain the impact of quota elimination on individual countries. These studies reflect a range of methodologies: some conducted original research, many cite existing studies, and some are based on the opinions of industry leaders and academic experts. Several refer to the testimony of government officials, experts, labour leaders and industry representatives at hearings conducted by the United States International Trade Commission (USITC) concerning the competitiveness of the textile and apparel industries in 2003.[52] Although some of the studies and reports attempt to assess impacts neutrally, most are far from disinterested.[53] While their conclusions should not be taken as definitive, they represent the current state of thinking among those who have taken a close look at the ATC, its expiry and associated effects.

These accounts do not always agree with global simulation models or with one another. Many contain recommendations for improving the competitiveness of a country's apparel industry. Given the diversity of methodologies and the general lack of comprehensive information pertaining to the role of foreign affiliates in the selected countries, it was not possible to treat every country in a systematic and harmonized fashion. Rather, the following review should be seen as a stock-taking based on the available evidence – which remains limited. This also means that the selection of cases reflects not only the importance of textiles and clothing in each country's economy and export performance but also data availability.

1. Africa

During the period 2002–2004, two thirds of all FDI projects related to the manufacturing of textiles and clothing products in Africa went to Morocco (6 projects), South Africa (3) and Mozambique and Swaziland (2).[54] Among sub-Saharan countries, the leading suppliers of apparel to the United States in 2004 were Lesotho, Madagascar, Kenya, Mauritius, Swaziland and South Africa.[55] According to Gibbon, who has conducted extensive research on the textile and apparel industries in sub-Saharan Africa, foreign affiliates account for a very important share of exports.[56] Foreign production in these countries is mainly controlled from Hong Kong (China) in Mauritius/Madagascar and from Taiwan Province of China and (to a lesser extent) Malaysia in southern Africa.

Evidence from Mauritius…Lesotho, South Africa and Madagascar points in a single direction. Increases in production for the United States market are mainly accounted for by firms that are Far Eastern–owned, specialised assemblers and finishers of long runs of basic garments. Where non–Far Eastern–owned enterprises also export significant volumes to the United States market, they normally share most of these characteristics except ownership… Finally, as the South African case shows, enterprises of the "Far Eastern" type seem to be able to produce profitably for the United States market even in the absence of qualifying for the trade preferences conferred by AGOA (Gibbon 2003a: 1821).

With regard to US manufacturers and retailers, African suppliers (like all suppliers) have had to engage in footloose "production migration" – that is, they have had to pursue "a trajectory corresponding to buyers' own migrations", becoming global contract manufacturers (GCMs) (Gibbon 2003a: 1822).[57] One South African producer described his plant (which exported primarily to the United States) as a "caravan", claiming that it looks exactly the same as the ones in Central America and mainland China: "Our objective has been that we could pack it up and unpack it wherever we needed to put it" (Gibbon 2003a: 1823).

Production in Africa has been strongly affected by AGOA, which provides tariff and quota exemption for African exports that meet specific rules of origin requirements (Bora, Cernat and Turrini 2002).[58] The least developed beneficiary country (LDBC) provision, which applies to countries that had per-capita incomes below $1,500 in 1998, provides the most significant preferences, permitting access to US markets on the basis of a "single-stage" rule – that is, preferential treatment requires only that final assembly be in the country of origin, regardless of where yarn spinning or fabric weaving or knitting occurs (Gibbon 2003a).[59]

AGOA sets quota ceilings for aggregate African apparel imports when third-country fabrics are used, although most AGOA countries do not typically utilize their full quota and so are unlikely to be affected. Apparel made in qualifying sub-Saharan African countries from domestically produced fabric and yarns, or from fabrics and yarns sourced from other AGOA-beneficiary countries in sub-Saharan Africa, can be imported duty-free but is subject to certain quotas (AGOA 2003). There is also a requirement that beneficiary countries "meet the requirement of an effective visa system and enforcement mechanism" to avoid illegal transshipments (Bora, Cernat and Turrini 2002: 29–30). Some 23 countries met these requirements as of January 2004. The ability to make duty-free imports is significant, since US tariffs average 17% of landed value, with cottons averaging 13% and synthetics 25% (Gibbon 2003a). In July 2004, AGOA was extended to 2015, and the special "third-country fabric" rule until 30 September 2007.

AGOA has had a significant impact on FDI and on apparel exports. US imports from Kenya, Lesotho, Madagascar, Mauritius and South Africa increased by 66% between 1999 (pre-AGOA) and 2001, to the point where they accounted for more than 90% of total African apparel exports. By way of comparison, imports to the EU from the five countries increased only 6% between 1999 and 2001. Growth reached 85% between 1999 and 2002, the most recent year for which data are available. Most of the growth in US imports was from Lesotho and Kenya. The growth in US imports resulted from increased capacity in the exporting countries,

rather than a shift in exports from the EU to the United States (Gibbon 2003a).

AGOA notwithstanding, it seems likely that African countries will be hurt post-ATC. AGOA is still in an early phase, and most African-based exporters do not yet have the economies of scale to compete effectively with more developed apparel industries (such as those in China). On the other hand, a study conducted for UNCTAD and the WTO (Hyvärinen 2001: 3) concluded that

> Mauritius has gained a strong position in the world markets for high-quality knitted goods and no doubt will continue to do so. At the same time there seems to be a ripple effect into other countries in the region. The production capacity in Mauritius is limited and therefore the overflow is being directed to Madagascar and some countries in East Africa… To sum up, there seem to be good possibilities for Mauritius, Morocco, Tunisia and Madagascar in the clothing sector. South Africa, Zambia, Uganda, Egypt and Senegal may also be able to compete in the post-ATC era.

The impact of quota phase-out may be mitigated by the recent extension of the LDBC provision on the rules of origin, since restricting preferential benefits to apparel made from US or sub-Saharan yarns and fabrics will result in high-cost inputs that will make the industries non-competitive.

The anticipated adverse impacts of quota phase-out will be worsened by the possible elimination of tariffs altogether by 2015. As Usha Jeetah, Mauritius's Ambassador to the United States, puts it:

> The proposals by both the United States and the EU to bring down their tariffs by 2015 will also contribute to the destruction of small and nascent apparel and textile industries in Africa. Both the United States and the EU have had hundreds of years to develop their apparel and textile industries protected by very high tariff barriers and quotas. What is being asked of the small and infant industries in Africa is that they will have 10 years in which to develop

their textile and apparel capacity to be competitive with long established countries with huge export capacities (Jeetah 2003: 2).

In addition to the sub-Saharan suppliers, some North African countries, such as Morocco and Tunisia, are also important exporters of apparel. Following are brief case descriptions of South Africa, Lesotho, Madagascar, Kenya, Mauritius and Tunisia.

a.   *South Africa*

Textile production in South Africa peaked in 1997 but fell off for several years thereafter, in part because of weak domestic demand. Textile imports have increased steadily, from 29% of total domestic textile consumption in 1991 to 37% in 2001 (Roberts and Thoburn 2003, Table 4). Only a small number of South African–owned textile firms are oriented primarily towards exports. In one survey of textile firms, while more than half reported exporting, for most the activity involved only a small percentage of their total production. Firms reported avoiding the export market because of the risks involved. The exceptions are a number of larger firms, based in Hong Kong (China) and Taiwan Province of China, that supply East Asian–owned apparel firms engaged in export primarily to the United States[60] (Roberts and Thoburn 2003).

Apparel production in South Africa is aimed at three principal markets: the United States; the lower-end domestic market (with some production also destined for the United States); and a mid-level domestic market (with some production destined for the EU) (Gibbon 2003a). The three main sourcing agents in South Africa are Linmark Westman International, Mast and Hot Source (Moodley 2002). J. C. Penney, for example, uses Linmark, part of the Taiwanese-owned, Singapore-based Roly International Holdings Group. Mast Holdings is owned by The Limited and is based in the United States; Hot Source is an Australian–United States–South African company. None of these companies engages in the production of apparel; rather, they provide global sourcing and supply chain management, including raw material and factory sourcing, product development,

production planning, quality assurance and shipping.

The three largest exporters from rural South Africa in 2001 were, from the eastern Cape, Ramatex Berhad (trading under the names May Garments and Tai Wah Garments), China Garment Manufacturers (CGM) and Tern Sportswear (in Kwazulu Natal). All three firms have engaged in backward integration in the region, investing in mills in order to obtain local sources of fabric (Ramatex in Namibia, China Garment Manufacturers and Tern Sportswear in South Africa) (Gibbon 2003a). Other large exporters are found in Newcastle (KwaZulu Natal) and in Botshabello and Qwa Qwa (Free State) (Gibbon 2003a).[61] Some European investment in textiles and clothing manufacturing in South Africa has been reported between 2002 and 2004 – for example, by Da Gama Textiles (Germany) in cotton production.[62]

US imports of textiles and clothing from South Africa have declined in recent years and stood at around $164 million in 2004. South Africa's future as an export base will depend partly on the value of the rand, which during the 1990s lost nearly 8% per year on average with respect to the dollar, significantly lowering the cost of exports.[63] However, while the exchange rate in December 2001 reached nearly 14 rand to the dollar, by early 2005 it stood at about 6 rand to the dollar, a level that may affect competitiveness.

b.   *Lesotho*

Lesotho's apparel industry was created in the early 1980s by South African companies searching for lower labour costs, for a way to avoid anti-apartheid sanctions, and for preferential treatment under the Lomé Convention's rules of origin for EU imports (which was available for Lesotho-based production). Today, however, the apparel industry is dominated by producers based in Taiwan Province of China (Table 15). This is especially true of the sector that exports apparel to the United States. The first such plant, Lesotho Haps, opened in 1986. During the next five years, additional factories included one from South Africa (jeans maker H D Lee, which later became part of Edgars retail group subsidiary Celrose), four from Taiwan Province of China, including China Garment Manufacturers (CGM) and C&Y Garments (owned by Nien Hsing), and one from Hong Kong (China). Production throughout the industry has since increased significantly, thanks in large part to AGOA.

Most employment is at a new industrial park outside Maseru, Ha Thetsane. By 2003, total employment had reached 40,000 in 54 plants. Table 15 lists the largest foreign affiliates in garment and shoe manufacturing as of 2002.

Table 15. Lesotho: largest foreign affiliates in garments and footwear, 2002

Company	Home economy	Industry	Employment	Entry year
Lesotho Precious	Taiwan Province of China	Garments	3,620	1999
Presitex	Taiwan Province of China	Garments	2,800	2000
CGM	Taiwan Province of China	Garments	2,000	1987
C&Y	Taiwan Province of China	Garments	1,900	1990
P&T Garments	Taiwan Province of China	Garments	1,840	2001
Nien Hsing Textile Co.	Taiwan Province of China	Garments	1,800	2001
United Clothing	Taiwan Province of China	Garments	1,700	1996
Evergreen Textiles	Taiwan Province of China	Garments	1,673	1995
Springfield Footwear	South Africa	Shoes	1,641	1995
Lesotho Fancy	Taiwan Province of China	Garments	1,540	2001
Tzicc	Taiwan Province of China	Garments	1,210	2000
Teboho Textiles	Taiwan Province of China	Garments	1,090	1997
Lekim	Singapore	Garments	1,071	1997
Tai Yuan	Taiwan Province of China	Garments	960	2000
Suntextiles	Taiwan Province of China	Garments	952	1994
King Ang	Taiwan Province of China	Garments	920	2001
Lesotho Hinebo	Taiwan Province of China	Garments	900	1989
N-River	Taiwan Province of China	Garments	850	2001
Hippo Knitting	Taiwan Province of China	Garments	850	2000
C-River	Taiwan Province of China	Garments	768	2001
Vogue Landmark	Taiwan Province of China	Garments	700	1996
Supreme Bright	Hong Kong (China)	Garments	635	2001
Superknit	Taiwan Province of China	Garments	600	1989
J&S	Taiwan Province of China	Garments	575	1996
Hong Kong Int.	Taiwan Province of China	Garments	550	2001
TW Garments	South Africa	Garments	500	2000
Carca Footwear	South Africa	Shoes	500	1997
Mountain Eagle	Fiji	Garments	490	2002
E-River	Taiwan Province of China	Garments	429	2001
Maluti Textiles	Taiwan Province of China	Garments	392	1998

Source: UNCTAD 2003a.

In 2002, about 30 foreign affiliates in the clothing and footwear industry accounted for 36,000 jobs in Lesotho (Table 15). Most of the clothing factories were owned by companies based in East Asia; 25 of the companies listed were from Taiwan Province of China, one from Hong Kong (China) and one from Singapore. Four of the factories in Table 15 were owned by South African companies. More than half of all the plants listed opened after 1999. In employment terms, the largest foreign clothing producers in 2002 were Lesotho Precious,

Presitex and CGM. Most workers in plants producing for the United States were engaged in making T-shirts, including the largest factory, operated by Lesotho Precious; the rest were mainly engaged in jeans manufacture. Principal consumers for Lesotho apparel exports include Old Navy (the Gap's low-end division), Wal-Mart and Kmart.

Lesotho is emerging as a major denim producer. CGM opened its Lesotho plant in 1987, the first denim manufacturer from Taiwan

Province of China in the country. Virtually all of its production is destined for exports, primarily to the United States (Laing 2001). Nien Hsing (Taiwan Province of China) is one of the largest apparel producers in Lesotho and the largest jeans maker in the world. It has engaged in upstream integration to provide its Lesotho production with locally produced fabrics. In 2001 Nien Hsing responded to AGOA by announcing plans for a new garment factory, scheduled for completion by June 2004, which would effectively increase Lesotho's monthly garment production from 3.9 to nearly 6 million square meters. This was expected to be Africa's largest vertically integrated denim fabric and jeans facility, complete with spinning, weaving, dyeing, finishing and sewing capacities, providing jobs for some 5,000 people (Laing 2001).

The Carry Wealth Group trades in Lesotho under United Clothing. In the view of the company's chairperson (Hendrawan 2003: 8), "By 2005, the phasing out of quotas will deal a blow to the industry with a flood of clothing imports to the United States from all member countries in the World Trade Organization around the world. Global competition will intensify and pressure on order prices and lead-times will be heightened. Countries with preferential trade deals with the United States will certainly be in a more favorable position". In anticipation, the company has moved production to countries that have preferential trade agreements with the United States, including AGOA.

Unlike in the case of South Africa, exports to the United States from Lesotho continued to grow rapidly in 2003, despite the fact that Lesotho's currency is pegged to the South African rand. In an interview in the *Financial Times* (14 September 2004), a leading Lesotho-based supplier insisted that it was still cheaper to export jeans to the United States from Lesotho than from China.[64]

c. Madagascar

The Madagascar apparel industry expanded rapidly in the latter half of the 1990s, when large Mauritian firms began producing in Madagascar in response to labour shortages and

rising costs in Mauritius. In 1997, Novel Denim Holdings and Crystal – two TNCs based in Hong Kong (China) and among the largest in Mauritius – opened plants in Madagascar. Novel closed its plant in 2002. Polo Garments Majunga, based in Belgium, is also listed among the foreign affiliates, with some 200 workers in 1999 (UNCTAD 2001b). Crystal makes knits, sweaters and wovens; it has plants in Mauritius and Madagascar, as well as China, Malaysia, Mongolia and Sri Lanka. Further outside investment came from the Gulf States, China and Sri Lanka (the latter from MAS Holdings, associated with Mast International, the principal sourcing agent of The Limited). By 2002, employment in the apparel industry had reached 80,000, with the average factory employing 1,500 workers (Gibbon 2003a). Gibbon (p. 1820), drawing on research by Tait (2002), concludes that "Mauritian-owned firms now accounted for 40% of employment, Far Eastern ones for 30%, Gulf states and South Asia for 20% and 'French and Malagasy' for 10%".

Madagascar apparel exports to the United States and the EU declined sharply in 2002 during intense social unrest, during which some Mauritian investors withdrew. However, exports to the United States recovered well in 2003, even though those to the EU did not. Gibbon argues that Madagascar exports to the United States are competitive and therefore should survive the end of the ATC.[65]

d. Kenya

There are about 21 garment factories employing as many as 30,000 workers in Kenya.[66] Principal producers include Kenya Altex (a Qatar-based joint venture between Global Readymade Garments and Industrial Promotion Services, an affiliate of the Aga Khan Fund for Economic Development), Tri Star (Sri Lanka) and Apparel Exports Ltd. (Sri Lanka) (Gibbon 2003a; East African Standard 2003). In December 2003, Kenya Altex opened its plant in the export-processing zone at Athi River, described as a "state of the art facility" that will employ 2,000 (mainly female) workers – a greenfield project that, according to the Aga Khan Development Network press release, "is purpose-built, has set benchmarks in technology, training and productivity. Its pioneering welfare and childcare facilities rank it as a regional industry leader" (AKDN 2003).

The Kenyan industry was convulsed by a major strike, including over union recognition, at the end of 2002 and the beginning of 2003. Whereas trade union rights had been pressed by the United States in relation to Swaziland's access to AGOA preferences, similar pressure was absent in the Kenyan case.[67]

Kenya is braced for the scheduled end of the LDBC provision of AGOA. Mukhisa Kituyi, Kenya's minister for trade and industry, told *Women's Wear Daily* that Kenya views AGOA

> not just as an opportunity to access a market, but also as a wake-up call to come to speed in a competitive global liberalized economy…as giving us an opportunity to quickly work on capacity and competitiveness, quality responsiveness to market requirements. You have to balance the principle of trade liberalization with the principles of developing capacity to adequately benefit from trade liberalization as an international agenda.[68]

Kituyi credits the near-quadrupling of Kenya's apparel employment in the past few years to AGOA and predicts a doubling of exports to nearly $250 million in the coming year – and a reversal of these gains if Kenya is required to produce from indigenous textiles in order to maintain preferential treatment.[69]

Kenya has attracted a few smaller Sri Lankan companies that are undertaking cut-make-trim of imported fabric for AGOA exports (UNCTAD, forthcoming). It is, however, not clear if they have the management and financial capacity to invest in the production of fabrics and accessories, entailing tens of millions of dollars of investment, or to create strong relationships with major brands and retailers. These conditions probably have to be met in order to survive over the medium term. Kenya may have started too late and too small to build an integrated apparel and textiles industry. Substantial fabric production has not begun. Kenya has not attracted the major apparel investors needed to create an integrated industry. Sri Lankan–owned garment producers are

already facing intense competition. One has shut down and two have amalgamated. One of the more successful Sri Lankan producers in Kenya is considering expanding but is likely to locate the expansion in either the Republic of Tanzania or Ghana.

e.   *Mauritius*

The apparel industry in Mauritius employs 15% of the country's workforce in 250 apparel-producing factories; an additional 5,000 people are employed in the textile industry, which provides fabrics for apparel manufacturing. The eight largest companies account for about half of all employment in the apparel industry, and most factories produce for the US or EU markets.

The industry was developed during the 1970s and 1980s by firms based in Hong Kong (China); although many of them are still operating, today the industry is Mauritian-dominated. The industry employs foreign contract workers (mainly Chinese women) as well as native workers. Foreign contract workers comprised a quarter of all workers in the large factories producing for the US market.[70] The largest producers for the US market are large branch plants (1,000–8,000 workers) of Hong Kong (China) or Shanghai-owned companies.

FDI, although modest in size; has played a central role in the development of Mauritius's textile and apparel industry in the country's EPZ. However, the FDI influx has proven to be short-lived, largely the result of efforts by US and EU firms to find new supply sources when constrained by quotas or other trade barriers. In recent years FDI has declined, and some foreign affiliates have closed operations. Among the companies departing in 2003 were the large Indian denim cloth manufacturer Arvind Mills, Texel Knitwear, Novel Garments, Winbright, Hong Kong Garments and Summit Textiles Ltd. All announced that they would close shop in Mauritius. In part these decisions reflected mounting competition from suppliers in Viet Nam, Bangladesh and Cambodia.[71] This trend is expected to continue post-ATC (Ancharaz 2003).

Appearing before the USITC (Jeetah 2003), Mauritius's Ambassador to the United States explained that the apparel and textiles industries account for 90,000 jobs and a quarter of the country's GDP. According to the testimony, nearly three quarters of apparel and textile exports go to the EU and a fifth to the United States. Apparel and textiles are the largest employer and the principal source of foreign exchange for the country and have enabled full employment, the empowerment of women, investment in neighbouring countries, and the transformation of Mauritius from an impoverished country in the 1970s to a model of sustainable development today. Despite rising labour costs and high transportation costs, Mauritius has remained competitive by investing in technology and skills training, moving into higher-value-added apparel production, and outsourcing lower-value-added activities to other African countries. Still, there is concern about the impact of the end of the ATC on Mauritius. While exports to the EU will likely be unaffected, one observer concludes that parts of the Mauritian industry selling into the United States are likely to disappear pretty rapidly.[72] In October 2004, the United States Congress voted in favour of an amendment to AGOA III giving Mauritius the "third-country fabric" exemption.[73]

f. Tunisia

Tunisia is among the largest exporters of apparel, which accounted for 37% of its total merchandise exports in 2003 (Table 2). It is estimated that foreign affiliates account for about 45% of total employment in the apparel and textiles industries.[74] Most exports comprise standardized garment production of relatively low value added. In recent years, Tunisia increased its share in clothing production, while higher-value-added activities related to textiles, such as spinning and weaving, declined in importance (IFM 2004). The trend towards specializing in lower-value-added production increases the risk that Tunisia will suffer from the phasing out of quotas. Its textiles and clothing producers now meet even more intense competition from Asian low-cost producers.

Tunisia is among the five largest suppliers to the EU of textiles and apparel.[75] The main competitive advantage of Tunisia vis-à-vis Asian countries lies in its preferential trading relations with the EU. However, without improvements in quality and a shift towards higher-value activities, this advantage risks being eroded over time. Tunisian producers face a number of short- and long-term challenges. In the short term, they may need to identify niche markets for their products and diversify their product range. The mentioned need for "lean retailing" may offer opportunities for Tunisian firms that are able to deliver small replenishment orders to the European market at relatively low transportation costs. In the longer term, the challenge involves technological upgrading towards higher-value-added activities including textile production and moving towards the development of "full package" supply. This will have to involve the strengthening of firms' technological capabilities through education and training.

2. Latin America and the Caribbean

Mexico, Central America and the Caribbean enjoy preferential treatment in the US market: NAFTA for Mexico, and the CBTPA for Central America and the Caribbean. In 2001, four fifths of all apparel exports from CBI countries to the United States fell under the CBPTA (Table 16), but this share is declining fast.[76] CBI countries doubled their share of US clothing imports between 1990 and 2002 (from 8.5% to 16.3%) (ECLAC 2004: 88). Yet it seems likely that many of these advantages will diminish somewhat with the end of the quota system. The USITC predicts that the Mexican apparel industry will decline owing to wage competition from China, especially in such sectors as men's underwear (USITC 2003).

In recent years both Mexico and the Caribbean Basin have lost US market share to China, Mexico more so than the CBI countries. Whether this trend will continue post-ATC is a matter of debate.[77] Evans and Harrigan (2004), for example, argue that the emergence of lean retailing during the 1990s has made timeliness (defined as a "short and reliable lag between order and delivery") more important than before, thereby favouring suppliers that are close to major markets (p. 11). They further argue that many apparel items are continuously reordered, requiring "rapid replenishment". Analysing data provided by a US department store chain, they estimate that "for high-replenishment products, proximity to the United States is equivalent to a 53 percentage point reduction in tariffs, while for goods with a replenishment percentage of 25% proximity is equivalent to a 20 percentage point tariff reduction" (p. 14). Evans and Harrigan conclude that geographical advantage will

Table 16. Share of total apparel exports from CBI countries to the United States that fall under the CBTPA shared production arrangements, 2001
(Per cent)

Country	Share
Costa Rica	96.5
Haiti	94.9
Jamaica	94.1
Dominican Republic	91.8
El Salvador	85.9
Honduras	85.0
Guatemala	48.4
Nicaragua	28.6
Other	79.2
Total	79.6

Source: ECLAC 2004, Table II.9.

remain even when trade policy is liberalized, suggesting that "even when the MFA is finally phased out, trade patterns are unlikely to return to where they were before NAFTA and the CBI" (p. 21).

Dee (2003: 1) challenges this conclusion. She acknowledges that, while a three-day shipping time from Mexico would seem to compare favourably with &é days from Hong Kong (China) or 15 days from China, the overall advantage lies in the ability to provide full-package production. This ability, which has been developed in Hong Kong (China), Taiwan Province of China and China over the past several decades, may neutralize Mexico and the CBI economies' geographical proximity to the United States (Dee 2003). Although some Central American and CBI countries (such as Guatemala, Honduras, El Salvador and the Dominican Republic) have increased their share of US apparel imports in recent years, all suffer from an inability to provide the kind of full-package production that permitted East Asia to

thrive in the past. It is estimated that only one third of the apparel industry in Central America and the Dominican Republic is equipped to move into full-package production by 2005 (Milian Jerez 2005). ECLAC (2004: 90) provides a succinct summary of the difficulties that may lie ahead:

In contrast, the situation of this industry in the small Caribbean Basin countries is very different. In general, the manufacturers operating in these economies are subsidiaries of foreign branded manufacturers (especially of women's undergarments) or domestic or foreign firms that compete for assembly contracts (particularly for men's wear) from large United States retailers. This is why the full-package concept has not flourished in the Central American and Caribbean countries, since their competitive advantages are derived strictly from the characteristics that make them well-suited to final product assembly: EPZs, preferential access to the United States and low wages.

In summarizing its review of Costa Rica, Honduras, the Dominican Republic and Jamaica, ECLAC (2004: 91–92) concludes that "the industry's future prospects – particularly in Honduras and the Dominican Republic, where it is still very important – are not very promising… [These countries] did not reach the level of industrial and technological upgrading needed to sustain exports, and some of these countries are caught in the low-value-added trap".

In terms of new FDI projects related to manufacturing of textiles and clothing in the LAC region, Brazil and Mexico have been the prime destinations in recent years, followed by Honduras and Nicaragua. Half of all such projects were undertaken by companies based in three locations: the United States, Taiwan Province of China and Italy.[78]

a. Mexico

Although Mexico has a number of large Mexican-owned apparel manufacturers, few of them are capable of even purchasing the textiles used in assembly. Rather, most are provided with piece goods by the firm placing the order. One reason for this is the high cost of credit (Bair and Dussel Peters 2004).[79] As a consequence, only the larger, more well-established (and typically foreign-owned) firms in Mexico – those with access to credit from US banks, or else substantial sources of their own revenues – are able to do their own textile sourcing.[80]

NAFTA's "triple transformation rule" (also known as "yarn forward") provided Mexico with preferential treatment for apparel and textile products that contained yarns made in any one of the three NAFTA countries. This in theory provided Mexico with an enhanced ability to export clothing made with Mexican fabrics. While a small number of integrated Mexican manufacturers did indeed benefit,[81] United States–based textile firms also saw an opportunity for vertical integration with Mexican manufacturers that might reverse their own long-term decline, and emerged as prominent players. Burlington Industries, for example, invested $80 million in five Mexican apparel plants, which it characterized as providing "one-stop shopping" for its clients (Bair and Gereffi 2003). Other US textile firms that invested heavily in Mexico included Guilford Mills, Malden Mills, Galey & Lord, Cone Mills and Dan River. As Bair and Dussel Peters note (2004: 20), "U.S. textile companies saw this strategy of forward integration as a way to shore up fabric sales to clients that might otherwise subcontract out production to Asian companies which are less likely to use U.S. fabrics". This strategy was not entirely successful, however: all of the above-mentioned firms have filed for bankruptcy since 2001, which in turn has impeded the expansion of Mexico's textile-producing capabilities (Bair and Dussel Peters 2004).

Among Mexican firms, Avante Textile, located near Mexico City, had a workforce of 5,000 in 2001. It was the largest vertically integrated Mexican manufacturer of knit fabrics, also specializing in yarn and apparel manufacturing and retailing. Avante produced about 3 million pieces each month, 30% of which went to US clients (e.g. J. C. Penney). The company is also a licensee for such brands as Disney, Warner Brothers and Skiny (a German company specializing in upscale undergarments). Kaltex, twice the size of Avante, is Mexico's largest manufacturer of woven fabrics and is considered one of Mexico's leading textile companies. In 1998 it was the largest Mexican consumer of US cotton. It has become one of Mexico's largest denim producers, exporting most of its denim to the United States through its affiliate Denimex. Kaltex sells finished jeans as well as denim; its principal client is VF Corporation, the maker of Lee jeans (Bair and Gereffi 2002).

By 1998, Torreón had emerged as "the new blue jeans capital of the world",[82] producing some 4 million pairs of jeans each week, and employing 65,000 workers in 350 factories. By 2000, some 20 labels were sourcing from the region, including major retailers (e.g. K-Mart, Gap Inc., J. C. Penney) and marketers (e.g. Tommy Hilfiger, Calvin Klein). While most of the plants were owned by foreign (especially US) companies, four were Mexican (Bair and Gereffi 2003). These included firms that had successfully moved up from simple assembly into more integrated production that encompassed both textile and apparel manufacture (although design and marketing, the most profitable activities, remained largely in the hands of US companies). For example, OMJC, the third largest manufacturer in the region, is a joint venture between US apparel manufacturer Aalfs and the (Mexican) Martín family. OMJC "distribute[s] the jeans directly to American stores and manages their inventory information" (Gereffi, Martinez and Bair 2002: 215). Kentucky-Lajat emerged in 1995 as a joint venture between Grupo Lajat (a Mexican firm that owns L. P. Gas) and Kentucky Apparel (a US manufacturer). In 1999, Grupo Lajat bought out its US partner.

The post-NAFTA growth in Mexican apparel production, exemplified by Torreón, may have proven to be short-lived, as is evidenced by Mexico's decreased share of US exports, as well as the closing of a number of plants in Torreón. Since 2000, US apparel imports from Mexico have declined from 13.6% of all apparel imports to 10.6% (Bair and Dussel Peters 2004).

There are several reasons for this. First, the country's apparel industry is heavily dependent on the US market and so has been adversely affected by the slow-down in the US economy (Bair and Gereffi 2003). Second,

Torreón's relative success is not being repeated elsewhere in Mexico, where Torreón's synergies between fabric suppliers and apparel firms are lacking (Bair and Dussel Peters 2004). Finally, because of the rapid growth in demand for production in Torreón, labour costs in the region have risen. US manufacturers and retailers such as Sun Apparel, Wrangler and Levi Strauss initially responded by consolidating their own operations, building their own assembly and laundering plants.[83] During the past few years, however, there have been reports that firms are relocating some of their production to China.[84]

It is difficult to forecast accurately the impact of the end of the ATC on Mexico. On the one hand, in 2003 some two fifths of Mexico's apparel exports to the United States were found in only two export categories: pants and shorts of woven fabrics for men and women, respectively.[85] Within these two categories, a significant portion consisted of blue jeans, a relatively heavy product whose high shipping costs favour close sources of supply. On the other hand, Mexico's lack of a domestic cotton industry, and resulting reliance on higher-cost US-made fabric, may undercut its competitiveness, since lower-cost cotton fabrics such as denim can be obtained in Asia, especially in China, India and Pakistan.[86] This would seem to further favour a shift in denim production to Asia.

Moreover, Mexico has been largely unable to take advantage of NAFTA to develop the kinds of full-package production capabilities that make production in China increasingly attractive. As Bair and Dussel Peters note (2004: 15):

Industry analysts interpret Mexico's loss of United States import market share to China as evidence that the country has failed to capitalize on the opportunities that NAFTA presented to become North America's premier supplier of full-package apparel, and this is particularly worrying for the Mexican industry as the benefits of NAFTA are diminishing, due to the fact that Mexico has already enjoyed virtually all of the competitive boost to be gained from the elimination of tariffs and quotas under the NAFTA phase-in schedule. The "NAFTA effect"

is also being eroded by progressive liberalization of trade in apparel products under the auspices of the WTO's Agreement on Textiles and Clothing.

b. *Dominican Republic*

More than four fifths of the Dominican Republic's export revenue comes from CBI-related free trade zones, in which 70% of all employees are in the apparel industry. The implementation of NAFTA in 1994 essentially stopped the growth of apparel exports from the Dominican Republic, which has seen its share of US apparel imports decline by half (to around 4%). Although implementation of the CBPTA in 2000 offered some options for a remedy, the agreement did not provide parity with NAFTA: duty- and quota-free treatment applied only to apparel with much stiffer origin requirements than NAFTA (Navarro-Bowman 2003: 3). More than 90% of apparel exports from the Dominican Republic to the United States fall under the provisions of the CBPTA.

As of December 2000, US producers dominated the Dominican Republic's EPZs, with some $747 million in investment. US firms were followed by domestic firms ($312 million) and by foreign producers from the Republic of Korea ($75 million), Panama ($36 million), the Netherlands ($8 million) and Taiwan Province of China ($6 million) (Mathews 2002).

The Dominican Republic's share of US apparel imports grew from 2.8% in 1990 to a high of 4.4% in 1998, after which it began a steady decline; by 2003 it stood only slightly higher than 13 years earlier (3.1%) (Bair and Dussel Peters 2004, Table 2). This decline has been accompanied by a parallel loss of manufacturing jobs in the apparel industry – from 152,000 workers in 2000 to 126,000 in 2002, a 17% decline in just two years (Navarro-Bowman 2003: 3). When quotas on cotton headwear were removed, the plants making these products shut down altogether (Navarro-Bowman 2003).

The rules of origin requiring the use of US-made fabrics to benefit from tariff preferences have reduced the incentive for the industry in the Dominican Republic to integrate vertically, which will prove an additional disadvantage post-2005 (USITC 2003). Because of the massive investments required, the apparel industry has been unable to integrate to include textile manufacturing and other parts of the supply chain. This leaves it less able to compete in a quota-free trading environment. The Republic of Korea, one of the primary foreign investors in the country, is unlikely to invest further, or maintain investments after the removal of quotas, unless a United States–Dominican Republic free trade agreement is arranged and implemented (Navarro-Bowman 2003). Although, as was noted above, the Dominican Republic has joined with the United States and five Central American nations in signing CAFTA, the agreement has yet to be approved by the legislatures of all seven countries.

c. *Guatemala*

Textile and apparel production in Guatemala supports an estimated 137,000 people in production, warehousing, shipping, logistics and other services; production is valued at $1.4 billion. The industry is likely to remain competitive post-ATC because of its special access to the United States, its proximity to that market, and "the high level of integration between the textile, apparel and retail industries in the United States and the companies that manufacture in Guatemala and throughout Central America" (VESTEX 2003: 1). Additionally, Guatemala has substantial artisanal exports that enter the United States under the GSP. Consequently, Guatemala's share of US apparel imports has increased steadily – from 0.8% in 1990 to 2.3% in 2000 and 2.6% in 2003 (Bair and Dussel Peters 2004, Table 2).

d. *Honduras*

Honduras has become increasingly important as a supplier of apparel to the US market, rising from thirty-fourth place among the top exporters in 1990 to fourth place in 2003. In 1990, only 0.4% of US apparel imports came from Honduras; by 2003 the figure was 3.8% (Bair and Dussel Peters 2004, Table 2). Garment

production (and export to the United States) plays a key role in the Honduran economy: in 2003, garments accounted for two thirds of all Honduran exports to the United States (Bair and Dussel Peters 2004).

In 2003, only 17% of workers were employed in Honduran-owned factories; more than half (53%) were employed in US-owned factories, and 15% were employed in Korean-owned factories. While a number of firms are engaged in simple *maquila*-type assembly work, the most dynamic segments consist of vertically integrated manufacturers that produce their own fabrics (Dussel Peters 2004). Table 17 shows the nine textile firms operating in Honduras as of 2003, seven of which were vertically integrated. The nearly 23,200 workers employed in these factories accounted for about a fifth of the total employment in the country's EPZs (Bair and Dussel Peters 2004). Moreover, only two of the nine companies are Honduran-owned; one is a joint venture between Honduran and US firms (Caracol Knits and Fruit of the Loom), one is owned by a Canadian company (Gildan), and five are from Asia (1 from China, 1 from Taiwan Province of China and 3 from the Republic of Korea). Bair and Dussel Peters (2004: 17) conclude that, "to a large extent, this set of vertically integrated manufacturers is responsible for Honduras's booming exports to the U.S. market in recent years".

The *maquila* sector, which mainly produces basic knit apparel, is threatened by price competition that is only likely to increase post-ATC.[87] The more integrated textile-apparel firms may fare somewhat better, but they (like the *maquila* sector) are hampered by their specialization in basic knit garments, which are vulnerable to low-cost competition. The apparel sector's dependence on relatively costly US fabrics creates an additional competitive disadvantage. Bair and Dussel Peters (2004: 21) conclude that "specialization in the commodity end of the market does not bode well for Honduran exporters, especially given the impending elimination of quotas in 2005, which is expected to increase dramatically the volume of apparel exported to the United States from low-wage countries in Asia".

Table 17. Textile and apparel firms in Honduras, 2003[a]

Company	Ownership	Textile employment	Textile production	Apparel employment
Textiles Río Lindo	Honduras	375	175,000 yards/wk.	0
Caracol Knits	United States/Honduras	770	1 million lbs/wk.	7,000
Gildan Activewear	Canada	500	1 million lbs/wk.	4,800
ELCATEX	Honduras	2,100	1.6 million lbs/wk.	4,022
Yangtex	Taiwan Province of China	217	462,000 lbs/wk.	1,200
ENINSA	China	40	150,000 lbs/wk.	347
Woong Chun[b]	Republic of Korea	550	450,000 lbs/wk.	0
Shin Sung[c]	Republic of Korea	240	302,000 lbs/wk.	747
Cottonwise Textiles[b]	Republic of Korea	264	431,200 lbs/wk.	0
Total		5,056	5.2 million lbs/wk. (knitted) and 175,000 yards/wk.(not knitted)	18,116

Source: Bair and Dussel Peters 2004, Table 4; orig. Dussel Peters 2004.

[a] This table includes all textile firms in Honduras at the end of 2003. At that time, there were four additional textile projects in the planning stages or under construction.

[b] These two firms are not vertically integrated manufacturers of apparel. Rather than converting the fabrics they produce into garments, they supply other apparel manufacturers.

[c] This firm was not operational in 2003.

3. Asia

Among Asian countries, all studies have predicted that China and India would benefit from the quota phase-out; with few exceptions, however, most studies also agree that Bangladesh and Nepal are likely to be hurt, while opinions are more mixed regarding Pakistan and Sri Lanka. One comprehensive region-wide analysis notes that the entire region (but especially the smaller countries) has been highly dependent on the quota system, which launched the garment export industry in some places, contributing to its rapid growth throughout the region. South Asia makes garments mainly for buyer-driven mass merchandise and discount chains, so it has little control over the return received on the products. Only India and Pakistan have raw materials such as cotton, but even in these countries some policies, such as those that discourage the use of man-made fibres, may prevent their optimal use.

In most South Asian countries, including India, FDI has generally played a limited role in the textiles and clothing sector. The region currently competes almost exclusively on the basis of low labour costs, and this will not be sufficient to retain production when the protection afforded by quotas is lost. As a result, the quota phase-out has increased the risk of job losses, wage cuts and job quality degradation. One study concluded that the region as a whole should integrate, supporting its apparel and textile industry by taking advantage of its sizeable local market as a hedge against the loss of exports, as well as developing intraregional trade agreements with the United States and EU (Joshi 2002).

a. Bangladesh

A number of studies have focused on Bangladesh, which has experienced explosive growth in its clothing exports. Despite quotas and MFN treatment in the US market, these grew from $1 million in 1978 to $4.1 billion in 2002. But in contrast to that of many other major exporters, Bangladesh's garment industry comprises mainly local producers; according to one estimate, apart from EPZs (where most FDI is concentrated), 95% of the country's garment factories are owned by local companies or families (Juststyle.com 2003b). FDI in general has declined in Bangladesh in recent years and totalled only $12.4 million for apparel and textiles in 2002 – less than 5% of total FDI. (As recently as 1999 the total was $81.8 million.) In a recent survey conducted by the Bangladesh Board of Investment of the 22 largest foreign investors, only one textile company was listed (Daeyu Bangladesh Ltd., in 21st place) (BOI 2003; UNCTAD 2001b). Moreover, during the period 2002–2004, only one new FDI project in textiles and clothing manufacturing in Bangladesh was recorded by LOCOmonitor, namely the investment by Raymond (India) in a denim fabrics factory.[88]

Bangladesh depends on the export of low-cost ready-made garments, a sector that employs 1.5 to 2 million people, 90% of whom are women (Khundker 2002; Shefali 2002; Kearney 2003a). Wages are among the lowest in the world, but productivity is also among the lowest, limiting any competitive advantage that might be gained from low-cost production. Yet, despite the low wages, employment in this industry has helped to alleviate poverty, as well as empower women in their domestic relationships (Khundker 2002).

The country's exports to the EU have benefited from GSP arrangements (which permit duty-free access) as well as EBA. Thanks to GSP, Bangladesh has doubled its production of export-quality knit and woven fabrics since 1998, reduced its lead times, increased its value added, and become more price competitive. Bangladesh has also benefited from generous quota allocations with the United States. 98 % of the country's exports are to the EU and the United States (Awal 2003).

Textiles and clothing accounted for 83% of the country's total merchandise exports in 2003 (Table 5; see also Kearney 2003a, 2003b). Only an estimated 25% to 30% of the value of woven exports is added in Bangladesh (Bow 2001: 15; Kearney 2003a). Bangladesh is threatened by current quota-free regional trade initiatives, especially NAFTA and CBI, as well as by high costs of doing business (Bow 2001).

The elimination of quotas should affect Bangladesh's apparel and textiles industries differently, according to at least one study (Spinanger and Verma 2003). The textile industry may do well as a source of fabric for the region; simulations forecast a 17% increase in textile exports. The apparel industry, conversely, is less likely to be able to face competition from India, Pakistan and China.

Problems include the following (Bhattacharya and Rahman 2000; Awal 2003):

- There is no indigenous cotton crop, and consequently an undeveloped domestic textile industry; this, in turn, prevents Bangladesh from fully benefiting from its membership in the South Asian Association for Regional Cooperation (SAARC).
- Infrastructure is inadequate, as reflected in congestion and customs delays at Chittagong port, poor telecommunications, uneven "professional office practices", and uncompetitive and unreliable energy supplies (Bow 2001).
- The EU gave Bangladesh (and other LDCs) a 12.5% tariff margin by removing duties on imports of clothing; this will soon be conditional on rules of origin that Bangladesh and other countries will have difficulty in meeting (owing to limited backward linkages).
- The end of the ATC may mean higher yarn and textile prices for Bangladesh if exporting countries redirect these products to their own garment industries.
- Bangladesh's long lead times (120–150 days, in comparison with, for example, 12 days in India) are a major disadvantage.

A number of solutions to some of these problems have been proposed; including the following (Khundker 2002; Awal 2003):

- Since importers, soon no longer constrained by quotas, will be driven to a greater extent by costs, efforts should be taken to integrate the industry vertically to shorten production time.
- Steps should be taken to diversify the industry and increase the portion of value added by Bangladeshi workers compared to the final product value.
- Improved productivity – achievable through training, organization and technology upgrades – is necessary for increased competitiveness. Nari Uddug Kendra (NUK – the Centre for Women's Initiatives), a development-oriented NGO working to promote women's rights and gender equity in Bangladesh, has done a study of

- retraining needs. NUK helped create the Bangladesh Garment Workers Protection Alliance (BGWPA) and has developed other strategies for coping with the challenges facing the garment industry (Shefali 2002).
- Continued favourable GSP treatment by the EU would help.

b.   Nepal

Nepal is another LDC for which a fair amount of research is readily available. The ready-made garment industry is relatively new in Nepal. The industry began to grow after 1983, when quota restrictions on India resulted in spill-over business for Nepal. By 1999, the garment industry had become the largest exporter in the country, and in 2003 it accounted for 35% of merchandise exports (Table 2). Nepal serves 12 quota categories covering both cotton and rayon products, most notably cotton shirts, terry towels and shop towels (Pant and Pradhan 2002). The industry accounts for about a quarter of Nepal's total export trade (Kearney 2003a) and is a major source of foreign income (Nepal News 2001). It is likely to be hard hit by the end of the ATC; for reasons discussed below, many SMEs may not survive (Pant and Pradhan 2002).[89]

Total FDI in Nepal has been low; it averaged just $8.3 million annually during 1990–2000, peaked at $23 million in 1997, and dropped precipitously to around $5 million only two years later. Manufacturing accounted for 43% of all FDI in 2001; about a quarter of all manufacturing FDI is in the textile and apparel industries, a relatively insignificant amount. The largest source of FDI is India, followed by the United States and China (UNCTAD 2003b).

The quota system, by providing large quotas that effectively insulated the industry from competition, enabled Nepal to become an apparel exporter. But this situation has also limited exports to the United States[90] and discouraged the industry from developing in such a way as to become competitive with large exporters. Nepal's apparel industry is inefficient and troubled by outdated manufacturing, poor logistics, harmful policies and geographic isolation. The cost of production in Nepal is reportedly as much as 25% higher than in India

and Bangladesh, the result of higher costs of transportation, labour, fabric and other raw materials. Nepal's lead time (the time from the date the order is placed to the date that goods are shipped) is three times as long as India's.

Nepal's garment industry has discouraged the development of a handloom textile industry, which might afford it a niche market involving unique Nepalese designs utilizing indigenous fabrics. Meanwhile, the relative competitiveness of Nepal's exports has been worsened by US trade preferences for African and Caribbean exports (Pant and Pradhan 2002; Shakya 2001; Nepal News 2001; Adhikari 1997).

Another factor likely to worsen the prospects of FDI in all industries, including the garment industry, is the steady increase in insecurity over the past year, with the Maoists blockading the capital Kathmandu in August 2004 and forcing a number of large foreign affiliates to close.

A number of recommendations have been made to improve the efficiency and competitiveness of the industry (Shakya 2001; Nepal News 2001; Pant and Pradhan 2002):

- Develop and implement a governmental Ready Made Garment promotion policy to foster a climate more favourable to foreign investment – for example, by upgrading skills and technology, improving domestic input linkages, increasing trade support services, enhancing trade financing, and providing incentives (e.g. reduced freight charges, export financing, removal of export duties and other taxes).
- Emulate recent developments from the industrialized countries (e.g. eco-friendly products, social clauses, social labels).
- Develop a labour policy relevant to garment exports, considering issues related to job security, labour strikes, export delivery, and international business cycles.
- Develop industries that provide fabrics and accessories, build dry ports, and establish an EPZ to implement incentives and develop ancillary industries.

- Intensify lobbying for the GSP facility in order to counteract the adverse impact of preferential trade agreements.

-

- Diversify the export market to reduce reliance on the United States – while at the same time seeking preferential access to the US market.

c. India

In 1960, textile and apparel exports accounted for a minuscule percentage of total manufactured exports from India; by 2003 they stood at 21% (Table 5). Much, if not most, of the labour involved in apparel production is in the informal sector and is therefore afforded little protection. The large majority of India's garment exports are knitwear, of which nearly three quarters is made of cotton. According to a question-and-answer discussion with the USITC (2003), India alone has the ability to be competitive with China.

Chadha et al. (2001) conclude that the quota phase-out will boost Indian GDP by 0.6%; Kathuria, Martin and Bhardwaj (2001) place the estimate at $2 billion annually. Unni and Bali (2000) argue that the phase-out should create opportunities for Indian textiles and clothing to grow, since the presence of high export tax equivalents on Indian garments and textiles indicates high demand beyond the quota allocations.

India's textile and apparel industries have historically suffered from a lack of competitiveness, although there are indications that the situation is improving. Spinanger and Verma (2003) identify a number of problems, including inefficiencies in terms of:

- international transportation, resulting in significantly higher costs than in China for shipping containers to the United States, as well as substantial delays (for example, it takes twice as long on average to ship from India to the United States as from Hong Kong (China) – 24 days as opposed to 12 days);
- domestic transportation, including poor roads, lack of expressways, and local

restrictions, which exacerbate delivery times;
- energy infrastructure, resulting in industrial power costs that are often higher than those of competing countries;
- finance, reflected in high interest costs;
- communications, including high-speed Internet access and faxing and email facilities (although these problems now seem to be largely resolved); and
- transaction costs, owing to cumbersome regulations.

An estimated four fifths of the Indian garment industry is found in the small-scale sector – tiny, family-run establishments with fewer than 10 machines and virtually no access to foreign capital. Until recently, policies favoured small firms, restricting certain forms of government financing to firms below a certain size. While the situation has changed (the woven garment industry was deregulated in 2000; knits in 2001), problems persist (Panthaki 2003). Small-scale production and the lack of modern equipment contribute to poor-quality fabrics, while government policies that favour cotton have slowed the development of synthetic and man-made fibres for export (Spinanger and Verma 2003).

Although FDI has historically been low in India's textile and apparel industries, the end of the ATC has been expected to increase FDI. Kathuria, Martin and Bhardwaj (2001) argue that India has the potential to benefit substantially from quota elimination in terms of increased market access, employment, output growth and productivity gains. This will only occur, however, if domestic reforms are implemented to streamline production and increase productivity, which will be necessary to enable India to thrive in a period of heightened global competition. The study suggests a number of domestic reforms, including:

- Eliminating taxes and concessions that favour decentralized production arrangements and subcontracting, which result in inconsistent quality as well as labour abuses.
- Ending the bias against man-made fibres, which are subject to special taxes, industrial licensing requirements and import duties.[91]

- Eliminating delays in shipping and customs clearance when imported fabrics are used in production.

Between 2002 and 2004, nine FDI projects related to manufacturing in the textiles and clothing industry were recorded by LOCOmonitor. For example, in September 2004, Carrera Holding (United States) announced a greenfield textile project in India to consist of seven units – three engineering plants to manufacture machines and robotics for garment manufacture; a finishing house; an industrial service; online accounting and retailing. The company had identified two possible locations, Coimbatore in the south and a SEZ near JN Port in Mumbai.[92] Most other FDI projects originated in Europe and only one had its origin in Asia.

d. Pakistan

The textile and apparel industries are central to Pakistan's exports, accounting for 70% of the total (Table 5), 1.4 million workers (approximately two out of five) and a quarter of the country's GDP (Kahn 2003). Apparel manufacturing is the single largest source of industrial employment in the country, employing mainly men (90%) as sewers, with women working in trimming and packing. Pakistan specializes in men's woven and knitwear (trousers and shirts), utilizing locally produced cotton. While this provides a degree of upstream integration, reliance on indigenous cotton inputs hampers the industry's ability to compete in man-made fabrics. A large number of products ranging from cotton yarn to ready-made garments are under quota restraints, implemented by a private-sector Quota Supervisory Council and product group committees. Pakistan's labour costs are among the world's lowest, but quality and productivity are also generally low. The principal markets are the United States and the EU (Manjur 2002; Kearney 2003a).

Pakistan's lack of product diversity and innovation could prove a liability post-ATC, although the country's Trade Minister, H. A. Kahn, has advocated full liberalization. He notes that Pakistan has already taken a number of steps to strengthen its competitive position (Kahn 2003):

A broad policy framework Textile Vision 2005 aims at making Pakistan a more viable, stronger and much more competitive textile industry, especially at the value added stages. For this over United States $2 billion have been invested over [the] last 3 years for restructuring of the textile industry as a whole. Emphasis is being laid on increasing the share of the downstream industry in the overall textile exports of the country, meaning greater value addition and taking advantage of the high "Integrated Textile Indigenisation Index". Integrated factory-mode production has greater chances in [the] mass market for clothing which demands consistent quality across huge volumes of [a] single item of clothing.

Furthermore, increasing the share of man-made fibre [MMF] based products in the downstream industry is being stressed. Pakistan is in the process of expanding the raw material base for the MMF sector by encouraging the production of Polyester staple fibre and other man-made fibres within the country. The aim is indigenisation for we believe that quota elimination will benefit those countries most that have a high indigenisation index in the cotton as well as the man-made fibre base.

In order to be fully competitive, Pakistan must offer greater product diversity, including expanding into the more profitable women's wear sector. Other measures that would promote Pakistan's apparel export industry include the development of regional trading blocs, more aggressive marketing, and liberalizing its import regime (Manjur 2002).

e. Sri Lanka

The Sri Lankan garment export industry experienced high growth after the 1970s and continues to be the strongest manufacturing industry in terms of its contribution to the GDP, exports, foreign exchange earnings, and employment generation. It comprises about 1% of the global export market and has historically enjoyed a favourable reputation. Success has been achieved partly through such supportive governmental policies as subsidies and duty rebate schemes, duty-free imports of machinery and raw materials, and lower corporate taxes. The protection afforded by the quota system has also contributed. Sri Lanka has had a particularly large share of export quotas, which has made it more dependent on the MFA than some other countries. By the end of 1998, about 5% of all workers were estimated to be employed in the garment sector, 87% of them female. The garment and textile industries contribute nearly half of the country's industrial production as well as exports (Udagedara 2003: 3).

FDI in garments has helped in the country's diversification of its manufacturing exports. Half of all FDI in manufacturing has gone into textiles and garment production (UNCTAD 2004d). The largest cumulative investments in textiles and apparel have their origin in the Republic of Korea and Hong Kong (China) (European Commission 2001).

The country has enjoyed relatively secure market access for the past two decades through bilateral agreements with the United States, the EU, Canada and Norway (Kelegama and Epaarachchi 2002). The United States alone accounted for nearly two thirds of apparel exports in 2003, the EU for most of the rest. The US market is aimed at discount and department stores such as Wal-Mart, Target, Macy's and J. C. Penney (Udagedara 2003: 7). More recently, two new markets have emerged – India and sub-Saharan Africa. The Indo–Sri Lanka Bilateral Free Trade Agreement (March 2000) permits 8 million pieces of garments at duty concession to the Indian market, while the United States Trade and Development Act (2000) resulted in the relocation of much of the Sri Lanka garment industry to sub-Saharan Africa, which enjoys preferential treatment under the Act (Kelegama and Epaarachchi 2002).

The Sri Lankan industry is, however, experiencing declining competitiveness owing to heavy reliance on quota categories, concentration on a few markets, lack of direct marketing links with major purchasers, and high dependence on imported inputs. Productivity is low and labour costs have been increasing, although workers still have low wages and cannot unionize. Additionally, few linkages between garment and

textiles producers have developed, with most textiles being imported (UNCTAD 2004a). The lack of backward linkages is "due to the high cost of investment required for the setting up of such operations and the relatively small domestic market. Sri Lanka therefore faces stiff competition from [exporters] that have well established backward linkage industries [such as Hong Kong (China), the Republic of Korea, Taiwan Province of China and China]" (Udagedara 2003: 10). Most garment manufacturers are geared to produce standard, low-value-added garments under export quotas.[93] As a consequence of these factors, garment exports have been shrinking in recent years, a process that will likely accelerate with the abolition of quotas, resulting in a significant loss of garment-related jobs and worsening conditions of work and pay in those that remain. The weaker, less competitive businesses may fail. Some surveys estimate that as much as half of the local industry may have to close (Udagedara 2003: 3).

The picture is not all gloomy, however. A few Sri Lankan companies are forming joint ventures with foreign companies with a view to establishing integrated units in selected upscale niches. MAS Holdings, for example, has grown to become one of the world's leading makers of undergarments, sportswear and leisure wear. The company now employs some 21,000 people worldwide and operates manufacturing facilities in 10 countries, all of them set up in strategic partnerships with brands such as Limited Brands, Sara Lee and Speedo.[94]

Moreover, in 2004, the European Commission decided to grant Sri Lanka additional preferences under the GSP's special incentive arrangements for the protection of labour rights, thus doubling the general GSP benefit. Sri Lankan exports thereby benefited from further tariff benefits as a reward for the country's attempts to clamp down on forced labour, employment discrimination and child labour, and to protect union rights.[95] In January 2005, the European Union decided to advance duty-free access for Sri Lanka under the so-called GSP+ scheme to support the country's economy, which is recovering from the tsunami disaster that took place in December 2004. Accordingly, some 7,200 products from Sri

Lanka (including garments) will enjoy duty-free access to the EU countries from 1 April 2005.[96]

To leverage positive developments and to address the challenge of intense competition, various policy recommendations can be considered. Sri Lanka needs to invest in technology in order to shift even more to higher-value-added products. As a first step, the Government has imposed a tax on garments to fund technological and skills upgrading in the industry. While this is seen as promising, some of the funds have been used for other purposes (Kelegama and Epaarachchi 2002; Dent and Tyne 2001). Some recommended additional steps include the following (Udagedara 2003: 18–21):

National economic policy

- Develop electronic data interchange at ports and customs, as well as a programme to reduce the cost of utilities.
- Establish Sri Lankan business associations in export markets to secure strong business contacts.
- Reform labour laws.
- Develop an infrastructure adequate to support efficient external and internal trade logistics.
- Enter into bilateral arrangements with importing countries for preferential treatment, in particular the United States (for example, extend GSP to apparel products originating in Sri Lanka on the basis of assembly of the final product).
- Encourage the provision of international technical assistance to companies that are likely to be adversely affected, enabling them to increase their capacity to absorb the displaced workers.

Industry- level strategic initiatives

- Improve market intelligence and develop professional marketing in existing markets.
- Increase productivity, especially in factories serving the low end of the market.
- Introduce design and product development professional courses for industry participants through universities.

- Invest in processing and manufacturing, marketing and information technology, thereby reducing lead times.

f. *Cambodia*

Cambodia – like its South Asian neighbour, Bangladesh – is heavily dependent on apparel exports, which account for 82% of total merchandise exports. (The figure for Bangladesh is 68%.) In contrast to its neighbour, however, the Cambodian garment industry is close to 100% foreign-owned, notably by TNCs based in East Asia (Stuart-Smith et al. 2004). At the same time, FDI in 2002 totalled only $14 million in textiles and $13.6 million in apparel, a substantial decline from three years earlier (in 1999, the corresponding figures were $57.8 million and $60.8 million). Among the foreign firms that have invested in the past few years in the textile and apparel industries are June Textiles (China), YGM and Gennon Garment Manufacturing (Hong Kong, China), M&V Industrial Manufacturing (Macao, China), King First International (Taiwan Province of China), Hytex Integrated (Malaysia) and Fast Retailing (Japan) (UNCTAD 2003c; LOCOmonitor).

The United States accounts for two thirds of Cambodia's apparel exports, which quadrupled (to $1.5 billion) between 1998 and 2003, rising 11% in the last year alone. Employment at the 200 or so factories has tripled since 1999 to 235,000 (mainly female) workers. The United States' largest apparel retailer, Gap Inc., accounts for some 40% of Cambodia's exports, primarily for its Banana Republic and Old Navy lines (Brooke 2004).

Cambodia's dependence on the Gap is indicative of the country's vulnerability to quota phase-out: the retailer manufactures about one sixth of all of its clothing in China, and there is considerable concern that more production will shift to China. Production costs in Cambodia's apparel industry are reportedly 25% higher than in China, and transportation to foreign ports takes considerably longer. (The major seaport is more than 100 miles from Phnom Penh, where the factories are located; delays in shipping can be significant.)

Cambodia has been attractive for US manufacturers and retailers partly because it participates in an International Labour Organization (ILO) inspection programme designed to improve factory conditions. This programme, which was negotiated in conjunction with a bilateral trade agreement between the United States and Cambodia, has included preferential treatment in the form of extra quotas (up to an additional 14%). The higher quotas were directly contingent on such performance. Eleven field monitors working for the ILO make regular factory visits and publish an online report. Cambodian workers also have the right to strike and engage in collective bargaining, many are organized into unions, and an arbitration council provides dispute resolution (Brooke 2004).[97]

However, the elimination of quotas meant also that the labour rights portion of the treaty ceased to have an impact. Although ILO monitoring will continue, there are no longer preferential quotas as a reward for compliance, and so an important incentive for compliance has been removed. It remains to be seen whether US manufacturers and retailers will continue to be attracted by the ILO programme alone.[98] Meanwhile, clothing exports from Cambodia to the United States are not covered by the United States' GSP scheme and therefore meet import tariffs of about 17% (Stuart-Smith et al. 2004).

On 31 August 2004, Cambodia's legislature voted to join the WTO. Cambodia's ability to thrive post-ATC remains unclear: while apparel production has grown rapidly in recent years and the country's participation in ILO initiatives make it an attractive destination for investors, relatively high labour costs and infrastructural inefficiencies mitigate those advantages to an unknown degree.

Notes

[1] Excluding intra-EU transfers, the EU's exports of apparel amounted to $19 billion, or 8.4% of the world total.

[2] This section is based largely on Gereffi and Memedovic 2003.

[3] Bair and Dussel Peters (2004) compiled these data from official statistics of the United States Department of Commerce, US imports for consumption, customs value.

[4] China, Hong Kong (China), Taiwan Province of China, Macao (China) and the Republic of Korea.

[5] In terms of value, US apparel imports from Mexico declined from $8.7 billion in 2000 to $7.2 billion in 2003 (a decline of 18%); apparel imports from CBI countries declined from $9.7 billion in 2000 to $9.2 billion in 2003 (a decline of 5%) (Bair and Dussel Peters 2004).

[6] The imports to Hong Kong (China) mainly comprise goods in transit for re-exportation to the final destination.

[7] Wal-Mart alone – with revenues of $256 billion in the fiscal year ending 31 January 2004 – accounts for nearly a fifth of the total revenues of the world's 40 largest retailers (Appelbaum, forthcoming).

[8] In triangle manufacturing, a foreign buyer places an order with an East Asian firm (most commonly based in Hong Kong (China) or Taiwan Province of China) that it has worked with previously. The firm then arranges the production, either with factories in other countries that it owns or with factories that it contracts with. The factory completes the triangle by shipping the goods to the foreign buyer (Gereffi and Pan 1994: 127).

[9] There are other factors that make it less likely that other countries will be able to replicate the original East Asian experience. For a more complete discussion, see Henderson and Appelbaum 1992.

[10] These data are based on information provided by LOCOmonitor, a database developed by OCO Consulting covering over 26,000 greenfield and expansion projects (but not cross-border M&As). The database does not claim to be comprehensive. Information is obtained from over 6,000 sources including companies' press releases, government websites and the media.

[11] See, for example, "Top Form: The sexiest stock in town", *SBI Corporate Flash*, 18 February 2003; and "Top Form: Bra-vissimo", analysis by SBI, 24 April 2003, mimeo.

[12] Yue Yuen Industrial Holdings is the principal source of Pou Chen's shoe production; as of June 2004, Pou Chen held 50.1% of the stock in Yue Yuen (*www.yueyuen.com/investor_financial Highlights.htm*). Yue Yuen also has a network of more than 800 wholesale distributors and 250 outlets in China to distribute the branded products from Nike, Reebok, Adidas, and other labels made in its factories, and it has recently moved into apparel and sports accessory manufacturing (see *www.yueyuen.com/bOverview_businessDivisions .htm*).

[13] Yue Yuen website, *www.yueyuen.com/ bOverview_productionFacilities.htm*.

[14] According to the United States International Trade Administration, in its first two years AGOA helped to stimulate FDI of $12.8 million in Kenya and $78 million in Mauritius, and to create some 200,000 jobs in 38 beneficiary countries. See United States International Trade Administration (2002), *2002 Comprehensive Report on U.S. Trade and Investment Policy toward Sub-Saharan Africa and Implementation of the African Growth and Opportunity Act: The Second of Eight Annual Reports* (Washington, D.C.: Department of Commerce).

[15] Where quotas imposed a constraint, they were often traded, adding an estimated $1.50 to the cost of men's knit shirts, $5.25 to the cost of men's jeans, and $21 to the cost of men's suits (Gibbon 2003a).

[16] See "Cambodia's textile industry faces Vietnamese threat", *Asia Times Online*, 9 March 2001.

[17] "China's textiles industry creates opportunities for the world", *People's Daily* (overseas version), 31 January 2005.

[18] For a more detailed discussion see Esbenshade 2004.

[19] In practice, the quotas have acted as an export tax. They have been administered by the exporting countries. When quotas have been binding, quota rights have commanded a price, and in many countries these rights have been allowed to be traded. In order to export, a firm has had to either buy a quota in the market or forgo selling one it owns. The result is a cost to the firm similar to an export tax.

[20] The full text of the Agreement on Textiles and Clothing (ATC) can be found at *otexa.ita.doc.gov/atc.htm*; for a detailed explanation, see the WTO's website at *www.wto.org/english/thewto_e/whatis_e/tif_e/agr m5_e.htm*.

[21] While quotas have been phased out, tariffs remain. Tariffs on apparel are much less burdensome than quotas, however. The average US tariff on apparel is 17%, whereas the tariff equivalent of quotas – the amount of tariffs that would be necessary to produce the same restrictive effect as quotas – is estimated to be at least twice that amount, reaching 40% or more in the case of China and other Asian exporters (cited in Nathan Associates 2002: 11, 22).

[22] A quota was said to be "constraining" if it was 85% to 90% filled, although the EU used a 95% threshold (Nathan Associates 2002, note 7).

23   All countries are not equally pleased with this timetable. At an informal meeting of the WTO's Goods Council on 26 October 2004, seven developing countries and LDCs requested a special study on the adjustment costs arising from the elimination of quotas. The request was backed by Bangladesh, the Dominican Republic, Fiji, Madagascar, Mauritius, Sri Lanka and Uganda. Brazil, China, Cuba, India and Thailand opposed the proposal. (See "Textiles take centre stage at the WTO", *Bridges*, October 2004.)

24   By 2003, China's exports to the United States had increased to $11.6 billion, according to the United States Department of Commerce, Office of Apparel and Textiles.

25   AGOA authorizes the President of the United States to designate countries as eligible to receive the benefits of AGOA if they are determined to have established, or are making continual progress towards establishing, the following: market-based economies; the rule of law and political pluralism; elimination of barriers to US trade and investment; protection of intellectual property; efforts to combat corruption; policies to reduce poverty, increasing availability of health care and educational opportunities; protection of human rights and worker rights; and elimination of certain child labour practices (*www.agoa.gov*).

26   While the present report focuses on apparel, AGOA's most important economic impact is to give duty-free status to oil and oil product exports, which accounted for 84% of all US imports under AGOA in 2001 (Gibbon 2003a). For a detailed discussion of the impact of AGOA, see Mattoo, Roy and Subramanian 2002.

27   CAFTA was signed in 2004 by the United States, Costa Rica, El Salvador, Guatemala, Honduras, Nicaragua and the Dominican Republic (Polaski 2003a, 2003b). As of 23 March 2005, it had been ratified by El Salvador, Guatemala and Honduras.

28   The ATPA has been amended and expanded by the Andean Trade Promotion and Drug Eradication Act (ATPDEA) in 2002; it expires at the end of 2006.

29   Algeria, Cyprus, Egypt, Israel, Jordan, Lebanon, Malta, the Palestinian Authority, Syria, Tunisia and Turkey; Libya has observer status. See *europa.eu.int/comm/external_relations/euromed/free_trade_area.htm*.

30   See the Commission of the European Communities, "Green paper on the future of rules of origin in preferential trade arrangements", COM(2003)787 final, Brussels, 2003.

31   ASEAN countries have discussed maintaining quotas after 2005 and have explored the creation of a free trade area (USITC 2003).

32   The Trade Minister of Pakistan, H. A. Kahn (2003), in criticizing WTO anti-dumping measures, notes: "According to the International Textiles and Clothing Bureau, the textile sector has seen 197 initiations of anti-dumping actions from 1990 to 1999. From 1994 to 2001, the European Commission has been the biggest user of anti-dumping and anti-subsidy actions accounting for 64 initiations in the textile sector alone. Of these 57 were targeted against developing countries." He further notes: "The WTO Committee on rules and procedures is already debating the inadequacy of the anti-dumping law especially where the purpose behind initiation of investigations is simply to 'freeze' the imports."

33   It also sets a four-year limit on such protections, with provisions to extend this up to a maximum of eight years, "subject to a determination by competent national authorities that the measure is needed and that there is evidence the industry is adjusting" (WTO 2004b).

34   The authors attribute this to a stronger anticipation of quota phase-out by 2003, already incorporated into investment decisions, as well as recently negotiated trade agreements between the United States, Viet Nam and Cambodia (Spinanger and Verma 2003: 23). For a formal analysis of location determinants, see Appelbaum, Smith and Christerson 1994; for a more general discussion, see Bonacich and Appelbaum 2000.

35   Some also have weak labour laws and environmental protection, low tax burdens and strong restrictions on labour organizing (including the formation of independent unions) (see e.g. Tantillo 2003).

36   In one study, the general equilibrium model suggested that developing countries generally benefit in the long run through improved terms of trade and improved allocation efficiency (Bora, Cernat and Turrini 2002).

37   Full trade liberalization includes all tariff cuts, and services liberalization. For a detailed methodological discussion see Spinanger and Verma 2003, section II.

38   In their simulation, they also estimated the combined effects of the end of the ATC and full accession by China to the WTO, including all tariff cuts and services liberalization. This scenario had negative effects on textile exports for most countries (the principal exceptions were Japan and China).

39   When the effects of full China accession are modelled in terms of apparel exports, all countries (except China) are adversely affected.

40   One study estimated that the export tax equivalent of quotas in 1999 averaged 40% in the United States and 20% in the EU (Kathuria, Martin and Bharwaj 2001: 20). Another study concluded that tariff benefits were likely to be far less significant than quota benefits had been, since US textile and apparel benefits are "not prohibitive:" The average US duty on apparel items is 17%. This provides a thin margin of preference over producers not receiving preferential access – a margin that may in some

cases be less than the production cost advantages that large Asian supplies may enjoy vis-à-vis preferential suppliers in the Caribbean, Africa and Mexico (Nathan Associates 2002: 2). New trade negotiations are also likely to target peak tariffs on non-agricultural products.

[41] China is also taking steps to modernize its textile industry (fibres, yarns, fabrics), suggesting that even in this more capital-intensive sector, China may well increase its share of global production.

[42] Infant wear tripled in exports. J. C. Penney moved fabric-sided luggage manufacturing to China after quotas on this category were removed in 2002, and it plans to do the same with infant wear manufacturing currently being done in Thailand and the Philippines (USITC 2003). The significance of these shifts has been disputed, however. One source argues that these are all detail- and labour-intensive products that are favoured by Chinese manufacturing (McGrath 2003), while another claims that China's share of brassiere exports to the United States is merely proportional to its share of garment workers among developing countries (see Just-style.com 2003a). Restrictive rules of origin in CBI countries also have an impact.

[43] "China's textiles industry creates opportunities for the world", *People's Daily* (overseas version), 31 January 2005.

[44] Ibid.

[45] China's fabrics are imported primarily from the Republic of Korea, Taiwan Province of China and Japan.

[46] China's Accession Agreement with the WTO, WT/L/432, Section D.16.

[47] See e.g. "China relents, and promises textile tariffs", *The New York Times*, 13 December 2004.

[48] The export license system employed by the Ministry of Commerce is intended, among other things, to improve statistics, analysis and monitoring with regard to textiles exports.

[49] Personal communication by Peter Gibbon, December 2003.

[50] See, for example, "Top Form: The sexiest stock in town", *SBI Corporate Flash*, 18 February 2003; and "Top Form: Bra-vissimo", analysis by SBI, 24 April 2003, mimeo.

[51] The Fair Labor Association's members include 15 footwear- and apparel-related companies with sales totalling $30 billion, producing in 3,000 factories in 80 countries, as well as 191 colleges and universities (as of February 2005). Company members include Nike, Reebok, Phillips-Van Heusen, Liz Claiborne, Adidas-Solomon, Eddie Bauer, Patagonia, Nordstrom, Outdoor Cap, Zephyr Grax-X, Gear for Sports, Gildan Activewear, New Era Cap, Puma, Top of the World and Joy Athletic. The group's code of conduct can be found at *www.fairlabor.org/all/code/index.html*. The Worker Rights Consortium's members include

NGOs, independent labour rights experts, and 128 affiliated colleges and universities (as of 27 July 2004). Its code of conduct can be found at *www.workersrights.org/coc.asp*.

[52] USITC Investigation 332-448, *Competitiveness of the Textile and Apparel Industries*. Testimony and documents are available at the USITC website (*edis.usitc.gov/hvwebex//*) under the investigation number. (Registration, which is free, is required.)

[53] Most were conducted by, or on behalf of, countries and NGOs that are likely to be hurt the most by quota elimination; some were conducted by industry and other proponents of free trade.

[54] Data from LOCOmonitor.

[55] Data from the United States Department of Commerce, OTEXA. Product coverage: MFA.

[56] Personal communication by Peter Gibbon, December 2003.

[57] The phrase originates with Sturgeon 2002.

[58] See   again *www.agoa.gov/2003_eligibility_results.pdf*.

[59] Non-LDBC AGOA countries are subject to a "three-stage" rule – yarn spinning, weaving or knitting, and assembly must all occur in the country of origin, another AGOA country, or the United States.

[60] AGOA's requirement that apparel exports to the United States be made with African or US fabrics and yarns has encouraged such backward linkages, although only the East Asian–based textile and apparel firms, rather than domestic firms, appear to be taking advantage of this (Roberts and Thoburn 2003).

[61] According to Ramatex Berhad (2003), the company originated in 1982 in Malaysia as a small textile manufacturing plant. In 1989 it expanded vertically from dyeing and knitting mills into yarn manufacturing; and in 1992 it moved into finishing fabrics and printing. The company has been publicly traded (on the Kuala Lumpur Stock Exchange) since 1996. It describes its core business today as textile manufacturing and claims (on its website) to be the "undisputed leader" in Malaysia's textile industry, providing "a one-stop shopping centre that offers a wide range of textile products from yarn to garments". Although the company originated as a yarn and fabric manufacturer, it produces knitted garments (dresses, pants, T-shirts, polo shirts, etc.). Ramatex Berhad operates in China, Malaysia, Namibia and South Africa. It claims a global market share of 3% in its specialty, knitted tops (Gibbon 2003a). Neither China Garment Manufacturers nor Tern Sportswear maintains a public website, and no additional information was readily available on either firm.

[62] Data from LOCOmonitor.

[63] Personal communication by Peter Gibbon, September 2004.

[64] Personal communication by Peter Gibbon, September 2004.

[65] Personal communication by Peter Gibbon, September 2004.

[66] Estimates vary from 21,000 (Gibbon 2003a) to 30,000 (WWD 2003b).

[67] Personal communication by Peter Gibbon, September 2004.

[68] "Kenya's apparel ambitions", 27 May 2003, www.*sweatshopwatch.org/global/articles/wwdke nya_may03.html*.

[69] African countries with more advanced textile and apparel industries, such as South Africa and Mauritius, draw the opposite conclusion – that continuing preferential treatment for AGOA countries importing textiles from non-AGOA countries like China will only discourage necessary investment in domestic textile industries (WWD 2003b).

[70] Personal communication by Peter Gibbon, September 2004.

[71] See "Mauritius: Textile firms close down due to international competition", *BBC Monitoring Africa – Political*, 15 May 2003.

[72] Personal communication by Peter Gibbon, September 2004.

[73] See *www.agoa.info/?view=.&story=news&subtext =400*.

[74] "Le textile habillement tunisien à l'orée du big-bang ", Webmanagercenter, Tunisia, 3 January 2005.

[75] Today some 80% of Tunisian exports go to the EU, with the EU providing 71% of Tunisia's imports. For more information, see *www.europa.eu.int/comm/external_relations/tuni sia/intro/index.htm*.

[76] In 2004, the shares for selected countries were as follows: Costa Rica 86.1%; Dominican Republic 57.8%; El Salvador 36.4%; Guatemala 20.0%; Haiti 75.8%; Honduras 29.3%; and Nicaragua 6.7% (personal communication from A. Milian, February 2005).

[77] The research conducted at the Harvard Center for Textile and Apparel Research (HCTAR) challenges the conventional wisdom that Mexico and the CBI countries will lose ground to China in a post-ATC world, arguing that, because of faster turnaround times they will remain competitive in the replenishment items in which they currently specialize. See, for example, the presentation by Weil 2004.

[78] Data from LOCOmonitor.

[79] Factoring and letters of credit are less common in Mexico than in Asia.

[80] While a number of Mexican firms claim to engage in "full-package" production, the meaning of the term is somewhat vague in Mexico. While occasionally it is used to refer to Asian-style full-package production (whereby the firm receiving the order takes care of everything), most commonly it refers to the situation in which the manufacturer receiving the order purchases the textiles instead of being provided with the piece goods by the firm placing the order. As is noted in the text, few Mexican manufacturers can afford even this more restricted form of full-package production. Some former *maquiladoras* refer to anything other than traditional assembly subcontracting as full-package (i.e. if they cut the fabrics themselves, or finish the assembled garment in any way, such as laundering), but this meaning of the term is falling out of use (Jennifer Bair, personal communication, 26 August 2004).

[81] "Integrated" firms refer to those with relatively modern plans that encompass spinning and weaving through apparel production and finishing (Bair and Gereffi, 2003). This can be distinguished from "full-package" production, which also includes most or all of the activities involved in producing and delivering the final garment, from contributing to design specifications to providing fabric and other inputs to sewing, finishing, packaging, and shipping.

[82] The title of a chapter by Gereffi, Martinez and Bair, 2002.

[83] Sun apparel made its own jeans through an affiliate, Maquilas Pami. Wrangler built a new hub and plants in nearby towns. Levi continued to produce exclusively through contracting arrangements, by increasing its volume with major suppliers, such as Fábricas de Ropa Manjai (Gereffi, Martinez and Bair, 2002).

[84] Personal communication from Jennifer Bair, 26 August 2004.

[85] SITC codes 8414 and 8426 respectively.

[86] Bair and Dussel Peters (2004: 27) note that, unlike for Mexico and the CBI countries, where almost all exports in the yarn-textile-apparel commodity chain consist of clothing, "in 2003, apparel accounted for a much lower 63% of China's total exports in the yarn-textile-garment sector" (indicating the competitiveness of Chinese textile production).

[87] Bair and Dussel Peters (2004: 18) comment that "five years ago assembly contractors received $5 for a dozen t-shirts, while in 2003 they received $2.50. In 2004–2005, the price per dozen is expected to fall below $2.20."

[88] Data from LOCOmonitor.

[89] Nepal joined the WTO in April 2004, the second country to do so under procedures designed to help LDCs accede more quickly, thereby enabling them to enjoy the advantages of quota elimination under the ATC (Bradsher 2004).

[90] 90% of Nepal's apparel exports are destined for the United States (*Nepal News* 2001).

[91] Kathuria, Martin and Bhardwaj (2001) contend that, if such biases did not exist, India's textile and apparel exports would be 75% higher.

[92] Data from LOCOmonitor.

[93] 62% of total exports are under quota, mainly to the US market, although non-quota exports to the United States have been increasing. EU exports are largely non-quota (Kelegama and Epaarachchi 2002).

[94] See *www.masholdings.com*.

[95] See *europa.eu.int/comm/trade/issues/global/gsp/pr070104_en.htm*.

[96] See *www.lankanewspapers.com/news/2005/1/309.html*.

[97] A recent report found no forced labour, child labour or discrimination but did find evidence of involuntary overtime and poor payroll practices.

[98] Personal communication by Scott Nova, Executive Director, Worker Rights Consortium, 28 September 2004.

References

Abernathy, Frederick H., John T. Dunlop, Janice H. Hammond and David Weil (1999). *A Stitch in Time: Lean Retailing and the Transformation of Manufacturing – Lessons from the Apparel and Textile Industry*. Oxford: Oxford University Press.

Adhikari, Marina (1997). "The textiles and clothing sector. from MFA integration into WTO: Implications for Nepal." Copenhagen: University of Copenhagen, Economics Institute. Mimeo.

African Growth and Opportunity Act (AGOA) (2003). "About AGOA apparel trade quotas" and "AGOA's 'wearing apparel' rules of origin." *Agoa.info* website.

Aga Khan Development Network (AKDN) (2003). "President Kibaki and Aga Khan open state of the art apparel plant in Kenya." Press release. 19 December. *www.akdn.org*

Ancharaz, Vinaye Dey (2003). "FDI and export performance in the Mauritian manufacturing sector." Réduit, Mauritius: University of Mauritius, Department of Economics and Statistics. November. Mimeo.

Andriamananjara, Soamiely, Judith Dean and Dean Spinanger (2004). "Trading apparel: Developing countries in 2005." Kiel: Kiel Institute of World Economics. Mimeo.

Appelbaum, Richard P. (2000). "Fighting sweatshops: Problems of enforcing global labour standards." 16 August. University of California, Santa Barbara: Institute for Social, Behavioral, and Economic Research. *repositories.cdlib.org/isber/publications/01/*

_____ (forthcoming). "Fighting sweatshops: The changing terrain of global apparel production." In Richard P. Appelbaum and William I. Robinson, eds., *Critical Globalization Studies*. New York: Routledge. pp. 369–378.

_____ and Gary Gereffi (1994). "Power and profits in the apparel commodity chain." In Edna Bonacich, Lucie Cheng, Norma Chinchilla, Norma Hamilton and Paul Ong, eds., *Global Production: The Apparel Industry in the Pacific Rim*. Philadelphia, PA: Temple University Press, pp. 42–62.

_____, David Smith and Brad Christerson (1994). "Commodity chains and industrial restructuring in the Pacific Rim: Garment trade and manufacturing." In Gary Gereffi and Miguel Korzeniewicz, eds., *Commodity Chains and Global Capitalism*. Westport, CT: Greenwood Press, pp. 187–204.

Awal, M. A. (2003). "Benefits of quota elimination? Strategies for industrial re-structuring." Presentation by the Chairperson of the Bangladesh Textile Mills Association to the EU Directorate General on Trade. Conference on "The Future of Textiles and Clothing Trade after 2005." Brussels, 5–6 May. *trade-info.cec.eu.int/textiles/index.cfm*

Bair, Jennifer, and Enrique Dussel Peters (2004). "Global commodity chains and endogenous growth: Export dynamism and development in Mexico and Honduras." New Haven: Yale University. Mimeo.

Bair, Jennifer, and Gary Gereffi (2002). "NAFTA and the apparel commodity chain: Corporate strategies, interfirm networks, and industrial upgrading." In *Free Trade and Uneven Development: The North American Apparel Industry after NAFTA*. Philadelphia: Temple University Press, pp. 23–50.

_____ (2003). "Upgrading, uneven development, and jobs in the North American apparel industry." *Global Networks* 3 (2): 143–169.

Bhattacharya, Debapriya, and Mustafizur Rahman (2000). "Seeking fair market access for Bangladesh apparels in the United States: A strategic view." CPD Occasional Paper No. 11. Dhaka: Centre for Policy Dialogue.

Board of Investment (BOI) (2003). "FDI inflow survey: Foreign direct investment in Bangladesh during 2002." Bangladesh Board of Investment. *www.boibd.org*

Bonacich, Edna, and Richard P. Appelbaum (2000). *Behind the Label: Inequality in the Los Angeles Garment Industry*. Berkeley, CA: University of California Press.

Bora, Bijit, Lucian Cernat and Alessandro Turrini (2002). *Duty- and Quota-Free Access for LDCs: Further Evidence from CGE Modeling*. Study Series No. 14. Geneva: UNCTAD.

Bow, Josephine J. (2001). "Bangladesh's export-apparel industry: into the 21st century – the next challenges." Asia Foundation. *www.asiafoundation.org/*

Bradsher, Keith (2004). "Trying to stay competitive, Cambodia joins the WTO." *New York Times*, 1 September.

Brooke, James (2004). "A year of worry for Cambodia's garment makers." *New York Times*, 24 January.

Chadha, Rajesh, Druisilla K. Brown, Alan V. Deardorff and Robert M. Stern (2001*). Computational Analysis of the Impact on India of the Uruguay Round and the Doha Development Round Negotiations.* Medford, MA: Tufts University, Department of Economics Working Paper. *ase.tufts. edu/econ/papers/200107.pdf*

Chandrasekhar, H. E. K. M. (2003). "The future of textiles and clothing trade after 2005." Presentation by the chairperson of the International Textiles and Clothing Bureau to the EU Directorate General on Trade. Conference on "The Future of Textiles and Clothing Trade after 2005." Brussels, 5–6 May. *trade-info.cec.eu.int/textiles/index.cfm*

China: Ministry of Commerce (MOFCOM) (2004). *China Foreign Investment Report 2004.* Beijing: MOFCOM.

Dee, Philippa (2003). "'Tight clothing: How the MFA affects Asian apparel exports by Evans and Harrigan': Comments by Philippa Dee." Cambridge, MA: NBER. Mimeo. *www.nber.org/books/ease14/dee11-7-03comment.pdf*

Dent, Kelly, and Mathew Tyne (2001). *Unraveling the MultiFibre Agreement: What Impact Will the Abolition of Quotas under the MFA Have on the Garment Industry of Sri Lanka*? Colombo, Sri Lanka: Transnationals Information Exchange, Asia.

Diao, Xinshen, and Agapi Somwaru (2001). Unraveling the MultiFibre Agreement (MFA): Impact of the MFA Phase-Out on the World Economy – An Intertemporal Global General Equilibrium Analysis. Washington, D.C.: International Food Policy Research Institute, Trade and Macroeconomic Division. TMD Discussion Paper 79 (October). *www.ifpri.org/divs/tmd/dp/papers/tmdp79.pdf*

Dussel Peters, E. (2004). *La Competitividad de la Industria Maquiladora de Exportación en Honduras. Condiciones y retos Ante el CAFTA..* Mexico City: ECLAC.

East African Standard (2003). "Aga Khan to hold talks with Kibaki." 18 December. *www.eaststandard.net*

ECLAC (2004). *Foreign Investment in Latin America and the Caribbean 2003.* Santiago, Chile: United Nations.

Esbenshade, Jill (2003). "Leveraging neo-liberal 'reforms': How garment workers capitalize on monitoring." Paper presented at the annual meeting of the American Sociological Association, Atlanta, Georgia. August.

_____ (2004). *Monitoring Sweatshops: Workers, Consumers and the Global Apparel Industry.* Philadelphia: Temple University Press.

European Commission (2001). *Guidebook for European Investors in Sri Lanka.* Brussels: European Commission Asia Investment Facility.

European Union (EU) (2003a). "Summary of studies and reports on the impact of textiles quota elimination." EU Directorate General on Trade, Background Paper. Prepared for the conference on "The Future of Textiles and Clothing Trade after 2005," Brussels, 5–6 May. *trade-info.cec.eu.int/textiles/index.cfm*

_____ (2003b). "Evolution of trade in textile and clothing trade world-wide: Trade figures and structural data." EU Directorate General on Trade, Background Paper. Prepared for the conference on "The Future of Textiles and Clothing Trade after 2005." Brussels, 5–6 May. *trade-info.cec.eu.int/textiles/index.cfm*

Evans, Carol L., and James Harrigan (2004). "Tight clothing: How the MFA affects Asian apparel exports." New York: Federal Reserve Bank of New York, International Research Department, 16 June.

Featherstone, Lisa (2002). *Students against Sweatshops: The Making of a Movement.* New York: Verso.

Flanagan, Mike (2003). "Apparel sourcing in the 21st century: The 10 lessons so far." Just-style.com, January. *www.just-style.com*

Francois, J. F., and D. Spinanger (2002). "Greater China's accession to the WTO: Implications for international trade/production and for Hong Kong, China." Paper presented at the Fifth Annual Conference on Global Economic Analysis, Taipei, Taiwan Province of China.

Gereffi, Gary, John Humphrey and Timothy Sturgeon (2003). "The governance of global value chains" (forthcoming in *Review of International Political Economy*). Sussex: IDS, University of Sussex. Mimeo.

Gereffi, Gary, Martha Martinez, and Jennifer Bair (2002). "Torreón: The new blue jeans capital of the world." In Gereffi, Spener and Bair, eds. (2002), pp. 203–223.

Gereffi, Gary, and Olga Memedovic (2003). *The Global Apparel Value Chain: What Prospects for Upgrading by Developing Countries.* Vienna: United Nations Industrial Development Organization. *www.unido.org*

Gereffi, Gary, and Mei-lin Pan (1994). "The globalization of Taiwan's garment industry." In Edna Bonacich, Lucie Cheng, Norma Chinchilla,

Nora Hamilton and Paul Ong, eds., *Global Production: The Apparel Industry in the Pacific Rim*. Philadelphia: Temple University Press, pp. 126–146.

Gereffi, Gary, David Spener and Jennifer Bair, eds. (2002). *Free Trade and Uneven Development: The North American Apparel Industry after NAFTA*. Philadelphia: Temple University Press.

Gibbon, Peter (2003a). "The Africa Growth and Opportunity Act and the global commodity chain for clothing." *World Development* 31: 1809–27.

_____ (2003b). "AGOA, Lesotho's 'clothing miracle' and the politics of sweatshops." *Review of African Political Economy* 30: 315–320.

Henderson, Jeffrey, and Richard P. Appelbaum (1992). "Situating the State in the East Asian development process." In Henderson, Jeffrey, ed., *States and Development in the East Asian Pacific Rim*. Newbury Park: Sage, pp. 1–26.

Hendrawan, Rusli (2003). "Chairman's Statement." *Annual Report 2002*. Carry Wealth Holdings Limited, 20 March. *www.carrywealth.com/ Annual_Report/2002/2002_AR_Eng.pdf*

Hilman, Jennifer A. (2003). "Will the benefits of quota elimination be spread evenly? Strategies for industrial restructuring." PowerPoint presentation by the Vice Chair of the United States International Trade Commission to the EU Directorate General on Trade. Conference on "The Future of Textiles and Clothing Trade after 2005", Brussels, 5–6 May. *trade-info.cec.eu.int/textiles/documents/118.ppt*

Hornbeck, J. F. (2004). "The U.S.–Central America Free Trade Agreement (CAFTA): Challenges for sub-regional integration." United States Library of Congress: Congressional Research Service. 1 June. *usembassy.or.cr/ Cafta/crstlc.pdf*

Hyvärinen, Antero (2001). "Implications of the introduction of the agreement of textiles and clothing (ATC) on the African textiles and clothing sector." Geneva: UNCTAD-WTO International Trade Centre. *www.intracen.org*

Institut Français de la Mode (IFM) (2004). "Study on the implications of the 2005 trade liberalization in the textile and clothing sector – consolidated report." Report for the European Commission Enterprise Directorate-General. *www.europa.eu.int/ comm/enterprise/textile/documents/ifm_final_rep ort_2005.pdf*

International Labour Organization (ILO) (2003). ILO Laborsta online database, Table 5B. *www.ilo.org*

International Mass Retail Association (IMRA) (2003). "Andean Trade Preferences Act renewal." *www.imra.org*

International Textiles and Clothing Bureau (ITCB) (2003). "Anti-dumping actions in the area of textiles and clothing: Developing members' experiences and concerns." Submission to WTO Negotiating Group on Rules (February).

Jeetah, Usha (2003). "Written statement in apparel and textiles industry in Mauritius." USITC Investigation 332-448, "Competitiveness of the Textile and Apparel Industries", 6 March.

Jones, Laura E. (2003). "Apparel and textiles: Assessment of the competitiveness of certain foreign suppliers to the United States market." Pre-hearing brief by the executive director of the United States Association of Importers of Textile and Apparel to USITC Investigation 332-448, "Competitiveness of the Textile and Apparel Industries", 8 January.

Joshi, Gopal (2002). "Overview of competitiveness, productivity, and job quality in South Asian garment industry." In Joshi, Gopal, ed., *Garment Industry in South Asia: Rags or Riches? Competitiveness, Productivity and Job Quality in the Post-MFA Environment*. New Delhi: ILO, pp. 1–11.

Juststyle.com (2003a). "World apparel convention focuses on quota freedom." Just-style.com, 8 July. *www.just-style.com*

_____ (2003b). "Garment industries in Bangladesh and Mexico face an uncertain future." Just-style.com, 20 October. *www.just-style.com*

Kahn, H. A. (2003). "Will the benefits of quota elimination be spread evenly? Strategies for industrial restructuring." Presentation to the EU Directorate General on Trade. Conference on "The Future of Textiles and Clothing Trade after 2005." Brussels, 5–6 May. *trade-info.cec.eu.int/textiles/index.cfm*

Kathuria, Sanjay, Will Martin and Anjali Bhardwaj (2001). "Implications for South Asian countries of abolishing the Multifibre Arrangement." Washington, D.C.: World Bank.

Kearney, Neil (2003a). "Trade in textiles and clothing after 2005." Presentation by the General Secretary of the International Textile, Garment, and Leatherworkers' Federation (ITGLWF), to the EU Directorate General on Trade. Conference on "The Future of Textiles and Clothing Trade after 2005." Brussels, 5–6 May. *trade-info.cec.eu.int/textiles/index.cfm*

_____ (2003b). "Disaster looms for textiles and clothing trade after 2005." Press release by the General Secretary of the International Textile, Garment, and Leatherworkers' Federation (ITGLWF). 9 February. *www.itglwf.org/*

*displaydocument.asp?DocType=Press&Languag
e=&Index=595*

Kelegama, Saman, and Roshen Epaarachchi (2002). "Productivity, competitiveness and job quality in garment industry in Sri Lanka." In Joshi, Gopal, ed., *Garment Industry in South Asia: Rags or Riches? Competitiveness, Productivity and Job Quality in the Post-MFA Environment.* New Delhi: ILO, pp. 187–215.

Khundker, Nasreen (2002). "Garment industry in Bangladesh." In Joshi, Gopal ed., *Garment Industry in South Asia: Rags or Riches? Competitiveness, Productivity and Job Quality in the Post-MFA Environment.* New Delhi: ILO, pp. 13–30.

Krishna, K., and L. H. Tan (1997). "The Multifibre Arrangement: Challenging the Competitive Framework." In Robertson, David, ed., *East Asian Trade after the Uruguay Round.* Cambridge: Cambridge University Press, pp. 59–77.

Laing, Lucy (2001). "Delighting in denim – a wonder fabric." *Pursuit: Clothing and Textile Magazine On-Line* (South Africa). August-September. *www.pursuit.co.za/archive/ augsep_denim.htm*

Malone, Scott (2002). "Who loses to China?" *Women's Wear Daily*, 26 November.

Manjur, Asir (2002). "Garment industry in Pakistan." In Joshi, Gopal, ed., *Garment Industry in South Asia: Rags or Riches? Competitiveness, Productivity and Job Quality in the Post-MFA Environment.* New Delhi: ILO, pp. 137–167.

Maquila Solidarity Network (2002–2003). "Memo: Codes update number 13: Where are we headed in 2003?" December-January. *www.maquilasolidarity.org/resources/codes/mem o13.htm*

Mathews, Dale T. (2002). "Can the Dominican Republic's export processing zones survive NAFTA?" In Gereffi, Spener and Bair, eds., *Free Trade and Uneven Development.* Philadelphia, PA: Temple University Press, pp. 308–323.

Mattoo, Aaditya, Devesh Roy and Arvind Subramanian (2002). "The African Growth and Opportunity Act and its rules of origin: Generosity undermined?" Policy Research Working Paper 2908 (October). Washington: World Bank. Mimeo.

Mayer, Jörg (2004). *Not Totally Naked: Textiles and Clothing Trade in a Quota-Free Environment.* UNCTAD Discussion Paper 176. Geneva: United Nations.

McGrath, Peter (2003). Testimony by the Chairperson of the Board of the United States Association of Importers of Textile and Apparel (USA ITA) before the United States International Trade Commission, Investigation 332-448, "Competitiveness of the Textile and Apparel Industries", 22 January.

Merk, Jeroen (2003). "The international production of branded athletic footwear." Brighton: University of Sussex. Mimeo.

Milian Jerez, Alfredo (2005). "Strengthening participation of developing countries in dynamic and new sectors of world trade: trends, issues and policies." Paper presented at an UNCTAD Expert Meeting on Developing Countries' Participation in New and Dynamic Sectors of World Trade, Geneva, 7–9 February. Mimeo.

Moodley, Sagren (2002). "E-commerce and the export market connectivity of South African garment producers: Disentangling myth from reality." Cape Town, South Africa: Human Sciences Research Council, Knowledge Management Programme. Mimeo.

Moore, Carlos (2003). "Statement of the American Textile Manufacturers Institute to the United States International Trade Commission." Statement by ATMI Senior Vice President to Commission Investigation 332-448, *Textile and Apparel: Assessment of the Competitiveness of Certain Foreign Suppliers to the United States*, 22 January. Washington, D.C.: USITC.

Nathan Associates (2002). *Changes in the Global Trade Rules for Apparel and Textiles: Implications for Developing Countries.* Arlington, VA: Nathan Associates. 20 November. *www.nathaninc.com*

Navarro-Bowman, Chandri (2003). "Statement by the National Council of export free zones and the association of free zones of the Dominican Republic (before The United States International Trade Commission, Investigation 332-448, *Competitiveness of the Textile and Apparel Industries Investigation* 22 January http://www.cnzfe.gov.do/; http://www.adozona.org/ing/members/miembros. asp).

Nepal News (2001). "Spotlight garment industry: Under threat." 27 July–2 Aug. *nepalnews.com*

Nordås, Hildegunn Kyvik (2004). "The global textile and clothing industry post the Agreement on Textiles and Clothing." Geneva: World Trade Organization. Mimeo.

O'Rourke, Mary (2000). Interview. *Bobbin,* 1 August.

OTEXA (1995). "Quota growth rates." Office of Apparel and Textiles. May. *otexa.ita.doc.gov/growth.htm*

Palpacuer, Florence, Peter Gibbon and Lotte Thomsen (2003). "New challenges for developing country suppliers in global clothing chains: A comparative European perspective." Sussex: Institute of Development Studies. Mimeo. *www.ids.ac.uk/globalvaluechains/ publications/ clothingchains.pdf*

Pant, Dinesh and Devendra Pradhan (2002). "Garment industry in Nepal." In Joshi, Gopal, ed., *Garment Industry in South Asia: Rags or Riches? Competitiveness, Productivity and Job Quality in the Post-MFA Environment.* New Delhi: ILO, pp. 83–115.

Panthaki, M. K. (2003). "Transaction costs in garment industry I." *Express Textile* 11 (September). *www.expresstextile.com/ 20030911/edit02.shtml*

Polaski, Sandra (2003a). "Central America and the U.S. face challenge – and chance for historic breakthrough – on workers' rights." Carnegie Endowment for International Peace, Issue Brief (February). *www.ceip.org/files/pdf/TED-CAFTA-and-labor.pdf*

——————— (2003b). "How to build a better trade pact with Central America." Carnegie Endowment for International Peace, Issue Brief (July). *www.ceip.org/files/pdf/TED_ CAFTA_Polaski_July_2003.pdf*

Ramatex Berhad (2003). Corporate website. *www.ramatex.com.my/*

Ricupero, Rubens (2003). "Will all developing countries benefit equally from textiles and clothing liberalization?" Presentation to the EU Directorate General on Trade. Conference on "The Future of Textiles and Clothing Trade after 2005." Brussels, 5–6 May. *trade-info.cec.eu.int/textiles/index.cfm*

Roberts, Simon, and John Thoburn (2003). "Adjusting to trade liberalization: The case of firms in the South African textile sector." *Journal of African Economics* 12: 74–103.

Shafaeddin, S. M. (2002). "The impact of China's accession to WTO on the exports of developing countries." UNCTAD Discussion Paper No. 160 (June). Mimeo. *www.unctad.org/en/docs// dp_160.en.pdf*

Shakya, Bijendra M. (2001). "Summary of Nepalese garment industry under changing global trade environment." Nepal: WTO Cell, Garment Association – Nepal. 26 December.

Shefali, Mashuda Khatun (2002). "Impact of international trade regime on female garment workers in Bangladesh." International conference organized by University of New England, Asia Center, Armidale (Australia), 3–4 October.

Slater, Pamela (2003). "Textile and apparel: assessment of the competitiveness of certain foreign suppliers to the United States." Written comments of consumers for world trade submitted to Commission Investigation 332-448, 4 February. Washington, D.C.: USITC.

Speer, Jordan K. (2002). "Sourcing in China: Firms discuss advantages, issues." *Bobbin*, 1 January.

Spinanger, Dean and Samar Verma (2003). "The coming death of the ATC and China's WTO accession: Will push come to shove for Indian T&C exports?" Kiel: Kiel Institute for World Economics. Mimeo.

Stuart-Smith, Keith, Rekha Dayal, Peter Brimble and Sam Holl (2004). "Cambodia's garment industry: Meeting the challenges of the post-quota environment." Manila: Asian Development Bank. Mimeo.

Sturgeon, Timothy (2002). "Modular production networks: A new American model of industrial organisation." *Industrial and Corporate Change* 11 (3): 451–496.

Tait, N. (2002). "Prospects for the textile and clothing industries of Madagascar." *Textile Outlook International* 98.

Tantillo, Augustine D. (2003). "Textile and apparel: Assessment of the competitiveness of certain foreign suppliers to the United States." Statement by the Washington Coordinator of the American Textile Trade Action Coalition (ATTAC) to Commission Investigation 332-448, "Competitiveness of the Textile and Apparel Industries", 27 January. Washington, D.C.: USITC.

Tanzer, Andrew (2000) "The great quota hustle." *Forbes Magazine*, 6 March.

Textiles Intelligence (TI) (2004). "Report summary: Trends in Japanese textile and clothing imports." *Textiles Intelligence* 111 (May–June).

Thun, Eric (2001). "Growing up and moving out: Globalization of 'traditional' industries in Taiwan." Industrial Performance Center Special Working Paper 00-004 (June.). Cambridge: MIT.

Truong, Dinh Tuyen (2003). "The future of textiles and clothing trade after 2005." Address by Truong Dinh Tuyen, Trade Minister of Viet Nam, to the EU Directorate General on Trade. *trade-info.cec.eu.int/textiles/ documents/152.doc*

Tyagi, Rahual (2003). "Apparel globalization: The big picture." *Bobbin*, 1 January.

Udagedara, Saman (2003). "Assess the textile and apparel industries of foreign suppliers pertinent to their adjustment to final phaseout of quotas." Statement of Sri Lanka ITC Study on January 2005 (from Sri Lankan Commercial Minister; revised statement). USITC Investigation 332-448.

United Nations Conference on Trade and Development (UNCTAD) (2001a). *World Investment Report 2001: Promoting Linkages.* New York and Geneva: United Nations.

_____ (2001b). "FDI in least developed countries at a glance." Geneva: UNCTAD.

_____ (2003a). *Investment Policy Review: Lesotho.* New York and Geneva: United Nations. UNCTAD/ITE/IPC/MISC/2003/4.

_____ (2003b). *Investment Policy Review: Nepal.* New York and Geneva: United Nations. UNCTAD/ITE/IPC/MISC/2003/1.

_____ (2003c). "UNCTAD WID Country Profile: Cambodia." Geneva: UNCTAD.

_____ (2004a). "Assuring development gains from the international trading system and trade negotiations: Implications of ATC termination on 31 December 2004." Note by the UNCTAD secretariat. TD/B/51/CRP.1.

_____ (2004b). *The Least Developed Countries Report 2004: Linking International Trade with Poverty Reduction.* New York and Geneva: United Nations.

_____ (2004c). *The World Investment Report 2004: The Shift towards Services.* New York and Geneva: United Nations.

_____ (2004d). *Investment Policy Review: Sri Lanka.* New York and Geneva: United Nations. UNCTAD/ITE/IPC/MISC/2003/8.

_____ (forthcoming). *Investment Policy Review: Kenya.* New York and Geneva: United Nations.

United States Office of the Trade Representative (USOTR) (2003). *First Report to Congress on the Operation of the Andean Trade Preferences Act as Amended.* 30 April. Washington, D.C.: USOTR. *www.ustr.gov/reports/2003atpa.pdf*

United States International Trade Commission (USITC) (2003). "Hearing on effects of the January 1, 2005 phase-out of textile/apparel quotas: Notes on Q&A with commissioners." USITC Investigation 332-448, "Competitiveness of the Textile and Apparel Industries", 22 January.

Unni, Jeemol, and Namrata Bali (2000). "Subcontracted women workers in the garment industry in India?" Working Paper 123. Gujarat: Gujarat Institute of Development Research, India. Mimeo.

VESTEX (2003). "Written testimony of commission of VESTEX before the United States International Trade Commission." Textile and Apparel of Guatemala (VESTEX). USITC Investigation 332-448, "Competitiveness of the Textile and Apparel Industries", 5 February.

Walkenhorst, P. (2003). "Liberalizing trade in textile and clothing: A survey of quantitative studies." Working Party of the Trade Committee. Paris: OECD.

Weil, David (2004). "What drives employment in the global textile and apparel industries?". Presentation at the Sloan Industry Studies Annual Meeting, Atlanta, Georgia 19–21 April.

Women's Wear Daily (WWD) (2003a). "U.N. study addresses quotas' end." 22 July. *www.sweatshopwatch.org*

_____ (2003b). "Kenya's apparel ambitions." 27 May. *www.sweatshop watch.org*

World Trade Organization (WTO) (2001). "Comprehensive report of the textiles monitoring body to the Council of Trade in Goods on the implementation of the Agreement of Textiles and Clothing during the second stage of the integration process." G/L/459, 31 (July).

_____ (2004a). "Textiles: Back in the mainstream." In *Understanding the WTO: The Agreements.* Geneva: WTO.

_____ (2004b). "Anti-dumping, subsidies, safeguards: contingencies, etc." In *Understanding the WTO: The Agreements.* Geneva: WTO.

Selected UNCTAD Publications on Transnational Corporations and Foreign Direct Investment
(For more information, please visit www.unctad.org/en/pub)

A. Serial publications

World Investment Reports
(For more information, please visit
www.unctad.org/wir)

World Investment Report 2004.The Shift Towards Services. P.468. Sales No. E.04.II.D.33. $75.
http://www.unctad.org/en/docs//wir2004_en.pdf.

World Investment Report 2004.The Shift Towards Services. An Overview. 54 p.
http://www.unctad.org/en/docs/wir2004overview_en.pdf.

World Investment Report 2003: FDI Policies for Development: National and International Perspectives. Sales No. E.03.II.D.8. $49.
http://www.unctad.org/en/docs//wir2003_en.pdf.

World Investment Report 2003: FDI Polices for Development: National and International Perspectives. An Overview. 66 p.
http://www.unctad.org/en/docs/wir2003overview_en.pdf.

World Investment Report 2002: Transnational Corporations and Export Competitiveness. 352 p. Sales No. E.02.II.D.4. $49.
http://www.unctad.org/en/docs//wir2002_en.pdf.

World Investment Report 2002: Transnational Corporations and Export Competitiveness. An Overview. 66 p.
http://www.unctad.org/en/docs/wir2002overview_en.pdf.

World Investment Report 2001: Promoting Linkages. 356 p. Sales No. E.01.II.D.12 $49.
http://www.unctad.org/wir/contents/wir01content.en.htm.

World Investment Report 2001: Promoting Linkages. An Overview. 67 p.
http://www.unctad.org/wir/contents/wir01content.en.htm.

Ten Years of World Investment Reports: The Challenges Ahead. Proceedings of an UNCTAD special event on future challenges in the area of FDI. UNCTAD/ITE/Misc.45. http://www.unctad.org/wir.

World Investment Report 2000: Cross-border Mergers and Acquisitions and Development.
368 p. Sales No. E.99.II.D.20. $49.
http://www.unctad.org/wir/contents/wir00content.en.htm.

World Investment Report 2000: Cross-border Mergers and Acquisitions and Development. An Overview. 75 p.
http://www.unctad.org/wir/contents/wir00content.en.htm.

World Investment Report 1999: Foreign Direct Investment and the Challenge of Development. 543 p. Sales No. E.99.II.D.3. $49.

http://www.unctad.org/wir/contents/wir99content.en.htm.

World Investment Report 1999: Foreign Direct Investment and the Challenge of Development. An Overview. 75 p.
http://www.unctad.org/wir/contents/wir99content.en.htm.

World Investment Report 1998: Trends and Determinants. 432 p. Sales No. E.98.II.D.5. $45.
http://www.unctad.org/wir/contents/wir98content.en.htm.

World Investment Report 1998: Trends and Determinants. An Overview. 67 p.
http://www.unctad.org/wir/contents/wir98content.en.htm.

World Investment Report 1997: Transnational Corporations, Market Structure and Competition Policy. 384 p. Sales No. E.97.II.D.10. $45.
http://www.unctad.org/wir/contents/wir97content.en.htm.

World Investment Report 1997: Transnational Corporations, Market Structure and Competition Policy. An Overview. 70 p.
http://www.unctad.org/wir/contents/wir97content.en.htm.

World Investment Report 1996: Investment, Trade and International Policy Arrangements. 332 p. Sales No. E.96.II.A.14. $45.
http://www.unctad.org/wir/contents/wir96content.en.htm.

World Investment Report 1996: Investment, Trade and International Policy Arrangements. An Overview. 51 p.
http://www.unctad.org/wir/contents/wir96content.en.htm.

World Investment Report 1995: Transnational Corporations and Competitiveness. 491 p. Sales No. E.95.II.A.9. $45.
http://www.unctad.org/wir/contents/wir95content.en.htm.

World Investment Report 1995: Transnational Corporations and Competitiveness. An Overview. 51 p.
http://www.unctad.org/wir/contents/wir95content.en.htm.

World Investment Report 1994: Transnational Corporations, Employment and the Workplace. 482 p. Sales No. E.94.II.A.14. $45.
http://www.unctad.org/wir/contents/wir94content.en.htm.

World Investment Report 1994: Transnational Corporations, Employment and the Workplace. An Executive Summary. 34 p.
http://www.unctad.org/wir/contents/wir94content.en.htm.

World Investment Report 1993: Transnational Corporations and Integrated International Production. 290 p. Sales No. E.93.II.A.14. $45.
http://www.unctad.org/wir/contents/wir93content.en.htm.

World Investment Report 1993: Transnational Corporations and Integrated International Production. An Executive Summary. 31 p. ST/CTC/159. http://www.unctad.org/wir/contents/wir93content.en.htm.

World Investment Report 1992: Transnational Corporations as Engines of Growth. 356 p. Sales No. E.92.II.A.19. $45. http://www.unctad.org/wir/contents/wir92content.en.htm.

World Investment Report 1992: Transnational Corporations as Engines of Growth. An Executive Summary. 30 p. Sales No. E.92.II.A.24. http://www.unctad.org/wir/contents/wir92content.en.htm.

World Investment Report 1991: The Triad in Foreign Direct Investment. 108 p. Sales No.E.91.II.A.12. $25. http://www.unctad.org/wir/contents/wir91content.en.htm.

World Investment Directories
(For more information visit http://r0.unctad.org/en/subsites/dite/fdistats_files/WID2.htm)

World Investment Directory 2003: Central and Eastern Europe. Vol. VIII. 397 p. Sales No. E.03.II.D.24. $80.

World Investment Directory 1999: Asia and the Pacific. Vol. VII (Parts I and II). 332+638 p. Sales No. E.00.II.D.21. $80.

World Investment Directory 1996: West Asia. Vol. VI. 138 p. Sales No. E.97.II.A.2. $35.

World Investment Directory 1996: Africa. Vol. V. 461 p. Sales No. E.97.II.A.1. $75.

World Investment Directory 1994: Latin America and the Caribbean. Vol. IV. 478 p. Sales No. E.94.II.A.10. $65.

World Investment Directory 1992: Developed Countries. Vol. III. 532 p. Sales No. E.93.II.A.9. $75.

World Investment Directory 1992: Central and Eastern Europe. Vol. II. 432 p. Sales No. E.93.II.A.1. $65. (Joint publication with the United Nations Economic Commission for Europe.)

World Investment Directory 1992: Asia and the Pacific. Vol. I. 356 p. Sales No. E.92.II.A.11. $65.

Investment Policy Reviews
(For more information visit http://r0.unctad.org/ipr)

Investment Policy Review – Algeria. 110 p. UNCTAD/ITE/IPC/2003/9. http://www.unctad.org/fr/docs//iteipc20039_fr.pdf.

Investment Policy Review – Sri Lanka. Forthcoming.

Investment Policy Review – Nepal. 85 p. UNCTAD/ITE/IPC/MISC/2003/1. http://r0.unctad.org/ipr/Nepal.pdf.

Investment Policy Review – Lesotho. 84 p. UNCTAD/ITE/IPC/MISC.25/Corr.1. http://r0.unctad.org/ipr/lesotho.pdf.

Investment Policy Review – Ghana. 98 p. Sales No. E.02.II.D.20. $ 20. http://r0.unctad.org/ipr/ghana.pdf.

Investment Policy Review – United Republic of Tanzania. 98 p. Sales No. 02.E.II.D.6 $ 20. http://r0.unctad.org/ipr/Tanzania.pdf.

Investment Policy Review – Botswana. 91 p. Sales No. E.01.II.D. $ 20. http://r0.unctad.org/ipr/botswana.pdf.

Investment Policy Review – Ecuador. 117 p. Sales No. E.01.II D.31. $ 25. http://r0.unctad.org/ipr/Ecuador.pdf.

Investment and Innovation Policy Review – Ethiopia. 115 p. UNCTAD/ITE/IPC/Misc.4. Free of charge. http://r0.unctad.org/ipr/Ethiopia.pdf.

Investment Policy Review – Mauritius. 85 p. Sales No. E.01.II.D.11. $22. http://r0.unctad.org/ipr/Mauritius.pdf.

Investment Policy Review – Peru. 101 p. Sales No. E.00.II.D.7. $22. http://r0.unctad.org/ipr/Peru.pdf.

Investment Policy Review – Uganda. 65 p. Sales No. E.99.II.D.24. $15. http://r0.unctad.org/ipr/UGANDA.PDF.

Investment Policy Review – Egypt. 113 p. Sales No. E.99.II.D.20. $19. http://r0.unctad.org/ipr/EGYFIN1.PDF.

Investment Policy Review – Uzbekistan. 64 p. UNCTAD/ITE/IIP/Misc.13. http://r0.unctad.org/ipr/Uzbekistan.pdf.

International Investment Instruments

International Investment Instruments: A Compendium. Vol. XII. 364 p. Sales No. E.04.II.D.10. $60.

International Investment Instruments: A Compendium. Vol. XI. 345 p. Sales No. E.04.II.D.9. $60.

International Investment Instruments: A Compendium. Vol. X. 353 p. Sales No. E.02.II.D.21. $60. http://www.unctad.org/en/docs/psdited3v9.en.pdf.

International Investment Instruments: A Compendium.
Vol. IX. 353 p. Sales No. E.02.II.D.16. $60.
http://www.unctad.org/en/docs/psdited3v9.en.pdf.

International Investment Instruments: A Compendium.
Vol. VIII. 335 p. Sales No. E.02.II.D.15. $60.
http://www.unctad.org/en/docs/psdited3v8.en.pdf.

International Investment Instruments: A Compendium.
Vol. VII. 339 p. Sales No. E.02.II.D.14. $60.
http://www.unctad.org/en/docs/psdited3v7.en.pdf.

International Investment Instruments: A Compendium.
Vol. VI. 568 p. Sales No. E.01.II.D.34. $60.
http://www.unctad.org/en/docs/ps1dited2v6_p1.en.pdf
(part one).

International Investment Instruments: A Compendium.
Vol. V. 505 p. Sales No. E.00.II.D.14. $55.

International Investment Instruments: A Compendium.
Vol. IV. 319 p. Sales No. E.00.II.D.13. $55.

International Investment Instruments: A Compendium.
Vol. I. 371 p. Sales No. E.96.II.A.9; *Vol. II*. 577 p. Sales
No. E.96.II.A.10; *Vol. III*. 389 p. Sales No. E.96.II.A.11;
the 3-volume set, Sales No. E.96.II.A.12. $125.

Bilateral Investment Treaties, 1959-1999. 143 p.
UNCTAD/ITE/IIA/2, Free of charge. Available only in
electronic   version   from
http://www.unctad.org/en/pub/poiteiiad2.en.htm.

Bilateral Investment Treaties in the Mid-1990s. 314 p.
Sales No. E.98.II.D.8. $46.

LDC Investment Guides

Guide d'investissement en Mauritanie. forthcoming.

An Investment Guide to Cambodia: Opportunities and
Conditions. 80 p. UNCTAD/ITE/IIA/2003/6

An Investment Guide to Nepal: Opportunities and
Conditions.   88   p.   UNCTAD/ITE/IIA/2003/2.
http://www.unctad.org/en/docs/iteiia20032_en.pdf.

An Investment Guide to Mozambique: Opportunities
and   Conditions.   72   p.   UNCTAD/ITE/IIA/4.
http://www.unctad.org/en/docs/poiteiiad4.en.pdf.

An Investment Guide to Uganda: Opportunities and
Conditions.   76   p.   UNCTAD/ITE/IIT/Misc.30.
http://www.unctad.org/en/docs/poiteiitm30.en.pdf.

An Investment Guide to Bangladesh: Opportunities and
Conditions.   66   p.   UNCTAD/ITE/IIT/Misc.29.
http://www.unctad.org/en/docs/poiteiitm29.en.pdf.

Guide   d'investissement   au   Mali.   108   p.
UNCTAD/ITE/IIT/Misc.24.
http://www.unctad.org/fr/docs/poiteiitm24.fr.pdf.   (Joint
publication   with   the   International   Chamber   of
Commerce,   in   association   with
PricewaterhouseCoopers.)

An Investment Guide to Ethiopia: Opportunities and
Conditions.   69   p.   UNCTAD/ITE/IIT/Misc.19.
http://www.unctad.org/en/docs/poiteiitm19.en.pdf.   (Joint
publication   with   the   International   Chamber   of
Commerce,   in   association   with
PricewaterhouseCoopers.)

Issues in International Investment Polices for Development
(Fore more information visit
http://www.unctad.org/iia)

The REIO Exception in MFN Treatment Clauses. 92 p.
Sales No. E.05.II.D.1.

Issues in International Investment Agreements
(Fore more information visit
http://www.unctad.org/iia)

State Contracts. 84 p. Sales No. E.05.II.D.5.

Key Terms and Concepts in IIAs: A Glossary. 232 p.
Sales No. E.04.II.D.31.

Transparency. 120 p. Sales No. E.04.II.D.7.

Incentives. Sales No. 108 p. E.04.II.D.6.

Dispute Settlement: State-State. 109 p. Sales No.
E.03.II.D.6. $15.

Dispute Settlement: Investor-State. 128 p. Sales No.
E.03.II.D.5. $15.

Transfer of Technology. 138 p. Sales No. E.01.II.D.33.
$18.

Illicit Payments. 108 p. Sales No. E.01.II.D.20. $13.

Home Country Measures. 96 p. Sales No.E.01.II.D.19.
$12.

Host Country Operational Measures. 109 p. Sales No
E.01.II.D.18. $15.

Social Responsibility. 91 p. Sales No. E.01.II.D.4. $15.

Environment. 105 p. Sales No. E.01.II.D.3. $15.

Transfer of Funds. 68 p. Sales No. E.00.II.D.27. $12.

Employment. 69 p. Sales No. E.00.II.D.15. $12.

Taxation. 111 p. Sales No. E.00.II.D.5. $12.

International Investment Agreements: Flexibility for Development. 185 p. Sales No. E.00.II.D.6. $12.

Taking of Property. 83 p. Sales No. E.00.II.D.4. $12.

Trends in International Investment Agreements: An Overview. 112 p. Sales No. E.99.II.D.23. $ 12.

Lessons from the MAI. 31 p. Sales No. E.99.II.D.26. $ 12.

National Treatment. 104 p. Sales No. E.99.II.D.16. $12.

Fair and Equitable Treatment. 64 p. Sales No. E.99.II.D.15. $12.

Investment-Related Trade Measures. 64 p. Sales No. E.99.II.D.12. $12.

Most-Favoured-Nation Treatment. 72 p. Sales No. E.99.II.D.11. $12.

Admission and Establishment. 72 p. Sales No. E.99.II.D.10. $12.

Scope and Definition. 96 p. Sales No. E.99.II.D.9. $12.

Transfer Pricing. 72 p. Sales No. E.99.II.D.8. $12.

Foreign Direct Investment and Development. 88 p. Sales No. E.98.II.D.15. $12.

B. Current Studies

Series A

No. 30. *Incentives and Foreign Direct Investment*. 98 p. Sales No. E.96.II.A.6. $30. [Out of print.]

No. 29. *Foreign Direct Investment, Trade, Aid and Migration*. 100 p. Sales No. E.96.II.A.8. $25. (Joint publication with the International Organization for Migration.)

No. 28. *Foreign Direct Investment in Africa*. 119 p. Sales No. E.95.II.A.6. $20.

No. 27. *Tradability of Banking Services: Impact and Implications*. 195 p. Sales No. E.94.II.A.12. $50.

No. 26. *Explaining and Forecasting Regional Flows of Foreign Direct Investment*. 58 p. Sales No. E.94.II.A.5. $25.

No. 25. *International Tradability in Insurance Services*. 54 p. Sales No. E.93.II.A.11. $20.

No. 24. *Intellectual Property Rights and Foreign Direct Investment*. 108 p. Sales No. 93.II.A.10. $20.

No. 23. *The Transnationalization of Service Industries: An Empirical Analysis of the Determinants of Foreign Direct Investment by Transnational Service Corporations*. 62 p. Sales No. E.93.II.A.3. $15.

No. 22. *Transnational Banks and the External Indebtedness of Developing Countries: Impact of Regulatory Changes*. 48 p. Sales No. E.92.II.A.10. $12.

No. 20. *Foreign Direct Investment, Debt and Home Country Policies*. 50 p. Sales No. E.90.II.A.16. $12.

No. 19. *New Issues in the Uruguay Round of Multilateral Trade Negotiations*. 52 p. Sales No. E.90.II.A.15. $12.50.

No. 18. *Foreign Direct Investment and Industrial Restructuring in Mexico*. 114 p. Sales No. E.92.II.A.9. $12.

No. 17. *Government Policies and Foreign Direct Investment*. 68 p. Sales No. E.91.II.A.20. $12.50.

ASIT Advisory Studies
(Formerly Current Studies, Series B)

No. 17. *The World of Investment Promotion at a Glance: A survey of investment promotion practices*. UNCTAD/ITE/IPC/3. Free of charge.

No. 16. *Tax Incentives and Foreign Direct Investment: A Global Survey*. 180 p. Sales No. E.01.II.D.5. $23. Summary available from http://www.unctad.org/asit/resumé.htm.

No. 15. *Investment Regimes in the Arab World: Issues and Policies*. 232 p. Sales No. E/F.00.II.D.32.

No. 14. *Handbook on Outward Investment Promotion Agencies and Institutions*. 50 p. Sales No.E.99.II.D.22. $ 15.

No. 13. *Survey of Best Practices in Investment Promotion*. 71 p. Sales No. E.97.II.D.11. $ 35.

No. 12. *Comparative Analysis of Petroleum Exploration Contracts*. 80 p. Sales No. E.96.II.A.7. $35.

No. 11. *Administration of Fiscal Regimes for Petroleum Exploration and Development*. 45 p. Sales No. E.95.II.A.8.

No. 10. *Formulation and Implementation of Foreign Investment Policies: Selected Key Issues*. 84 p. Sales No. E.92.II.A.21. $12.

No. 9. *Environmental Accounting: Current Issues, Abstracts and Bibliography*. 86 p. Sales No. E.92.II.A.23.

C. Individual Studies

FDI in Least Developed Countries at a Glance: 2003. Forthcoming.

Foreign Direct Investment and Performance Requirements: New Evidence from Selected Countries. 318 p. UNCTAD/ITE/IIA/2003/7. Sales No. E.03.II.D.32.

FDI in Land-Locked Developing Countries at a Glance. 112 p. UNCTAD/ITE/IIA/2003/5.

FDI in Least Developed Countries at a Glance: 2002. 136 p. UNCTAD/ITE/IIA/6. http://www.unctad.org/en/docs//iteiia6_en.pdf.

The World of Investment Promotion at a Glance. Advisory Studies, No. 17. 80 p. UNCTAD/ITE/IPC/3. http://www.unctad.org/en/docs//poiteipcd3.en.pdf.

The Tradability of Consulting Services. 189 p. UNCTAD/ITE/IPC/Misc.8. http://www.unctad.org/en/docs/poiteipcm8.en.pdf.

Compendium of International Arrangements on Transfer of Technology: Selected Instruments. 307 p. Sales No. E.01.II.D.28. $45. http://www.unctad.org/en/docs//psiteipcm5.en.pdf

FDI in Least Developed Countries at a Glance. 150 p. UNCTAD/ITE/IIA/3. http://www.unctad.org/en/pub/poiteiiad3.en.htm.

Foreign Direct Investment in Africa: Performance and Potential. 89 p. UNCTAD/ITE/IIT/Misc.15. Free of charge. http://www.unctad.org/en/docs/poiteiitm15.pdf.

*TNC-SME Linkages for Development: Issues– Experiences–Best Practices. Proceedings of the Special Round Table on TNCs, SMEs and Development, UNCTAD X, 15 February 2000, Bangkok, Thailand.*113 p. UNCTAD/ITE/TEB1. Free of charge.

Handbook on Foreign Direct Investment by Small and Medium-sized Enterprises: Lessons from Asia. 200 p. Sales No. E.98.II.D.4. $48.

Handbook on Foreign Direct Investment by Small and Medium-sized Enterprises: Lessons from Asia. Executive Summary and Report of the Kunming Conference. 74 p. Free of charge.

Small and Medium-sized Transnational Corporations. Executive Summary and Report of the Osaka Conference. 60 p. Free of charge.

*Small and Medium-sized Transnational Corporations: Role, Impact and Policy Implications.*242 p. Sales No. E.93.II.A.15. $35.

Measures of the Transnationalization of Economic Activity. 93 p. Sales No. E.01.II.D.2. $20.

The Competitiveness Challenge: Transnational Corporations and Industrial Restructuring in Developing Countries. 283p. Sales No. E.00.II.D.35. $42.

Integrating International and Financial Performance at the Enterprise Level. 116 p. Sales No. E.00.II.D.28. $18.

FDI Determinants and TNC Strategies: The Case of Brazil. 195 p. Sales No. E.00.II.D.2. $35. Summary available from http://www.unctad.org/en/pub/psiteiitd14.en.htm.

The Social Responsibility of Transnational Corporations. 75 p. UNCTAD/ITE/IIT/Misc. 21. Free of charge. [Out of stock.] http://www.unctad.org/en/docs/poiteiitm21.en.pdf.

Conclusions on Accounting and Reporting by Transnational Corporations. 47 p. Sales No. E.94.II.A.9. $25.

Accounting, Valuation and Privatization. 190 p. Sales No. E.94.II.A.3. $25.

Environmental Management in Transnational Corporations: Report on the Benchmark Corporate Environment Survey. 278 p. Sales No. E.94.II.A.2. $29.95.

Management Consulting: A Survey of the Industry and Its Largest Firms. 100 p. Sales No. E.93.II.A.17. $25.

Transnational Corporations: A Selective Bibliography, 1991-1992. 736 p. Sales No. E.93.II.A.16. $75.

Foreign Investment and Trade Linkages in Developing Countries. 108 p. Sales No. E.93.II.A.12. $18.

Transnational Corporations from Developing Countries: Impact on Their Home Countries. 116 p. Sales No. E.93.II.A.8. $15.

Debt-Equity Swaps and Development. 150 p. Sales No. E.93.II.A.7. $35.

From the Common Market to EC 92: Regional Economic Integration in the European Community and

Transnational Corporations. 134 p. Sales No. E.93.II.A.2. $25.

The East-West Business Directory 1991/1992. 570 p. Sales No. E.92.II.A.20. $65.

Climate Change and Transnational Corporations: Analysis and Trends. 110 p. Sales No. E.92.II.A.7. $16.50.

Foreign Direct Investment and Transfer of Technology in India. 150 p. Sales No. E.92.II.A.3. $20.

The Determinants of Foreign Direct Investment: A Survey of the Evidence. 84 p. Sales No. E.92.II.A.2. $12.50.

Transnational Corporations and Industrial Hazards Disclosure. 98 p. Sales No. E.91.II.A.18. $17.50.

Transnational Business Information: A Manual of Needs and Sources. 216 p. Sales No. E.91.II.A.13. $45.

The Financial Crisis in Asia and Foreign Direct Investment: An Assessment. 101 p. Sales No. GV.E.98.0.29. $20.

Sharing Asia's Dynamism: Asian Direct Investment in the European Union. 192 p. Sales No. E.97.II.D.1. $26.

Investing in Asia's Dynamism: European Union Direct Investment in Asia. 124 p. ISBN 92-827-7675-1. ECU 14. (Joint publication with the European Commission.)

International Investment: Towards the Year 2002. 166 p. Sales No. GV.E.98.0.15. $29. (Joint publication with Invest in France Mission and Arthur Andersen, in collaboration with DATAR.)

International Investment: Towards the Year 2001. 81 p. Sales No. GV.E.97.0.5. $35. (Joint publication with Invest in France Mission and Arthur Andersen, in collaboration with DATAR.)

Liberalizing International Transactions in Services: A Handbook. 182 p. Sales No. E.94.II.A.11. $45. (Joint publication with the World Bank.)

The Impact of Trade-Related Investment Measures on Trade and Development: Theory, Evidence and Policy Implications. 108 p. Sales No. E.91.II.A.19. $17.50. (Joint publication with the United Nations Centre on Transnational Corporations.)

Transnational Corporations and World Development. 656 p. ISBN 0-415-08560-8 (hardback), 0-415-08561-6 (paperback). £65 (hardback), £20.00 (paperback). (Published by International Thomson Business Press on behalf of UNCTAD.)

Companies without Borders: Transnational Corporations in the 1990s. 224 p. ISBN 0-415-12526-X.

£47.50. (Published by International Thomson Business Press on behalf of UNCTAD.)

The New Globalism and Developing Countries. 336 p. ISBN 92-808-0944-X. $25. (Published by United Nations University Press.)

World Economic Situation and Prospects 2002. 51 p. Sales No. E.02.II.C.2. $15. (Joint publication with the United Nations Department of Economic and Social Affairs.)

World Economic Situation and Prospects 2001. 51 p. Sales No. E.01.II.C.2. $15. (Joint publication with the United Nations Department of Economic and Social Affairs.)

D. Journals

Transnational Corporations Journal (formerly *The CTC Reporter*). Published three times a year. Annual subscription price: $45; individual issues $20. http://www.unctad.org/en/subsites/dite/1_itncs/1_tncs.htm.

United Nations publications may be obtained from bookstores and distributors throughout the world. Please consult your bookstore or write,

For Africa, Asia and Europe to:

Sales Section
United Nations Office at Geneva
Palais des Nations
CH-1211 Geneva 10, Switzerland
Tel: (41-22) 917-1234
Fax: (41-22) 917-0123
E-mail: unpubli@unog.ch

For Asia and the Pacific, the Caribbean, Latin America and North America to:

Sales Section
Room DC2-0853
United Nations Secretariat
New York, NY 10017
United States
Tel: (1-212) 963-8302 or (800) 253-9646
Fax: (1-212) 963-3489
E-mail: publications@un.org

All prices are quoted in United States dollars.

For further information on the work of the Division on Investment, Technology and Enterprise Development, UNCTAD, please address inquiries to:

United Nations Conference on Trade
and Development
Division on Investment, Technology
and Enterprise Development
Palais des Nations,
Room E-10054
CH-1211 Geneva 10,
Switzerland
Telephone: (41-22) 907-5651
Telefax: (41-22) 907-0498
E-mail: natalia.guerra@unctad.org;
Internet:http://www.unctad.org

QUESTIONNAIRE

TNCs and the Removal of Textiles and Clothing Quotas

Sales No. E.05.II.D.20

In order to improve the quality and relevance of the work of the UNCTAD Division on Investment, Technology and Enterprise Development, it would be useful to receive the views of readers on this publication. It would therefore be greatly appreciated if you could complete the following questionnaire and return to:

Readership Survey
UNCTAD Division on Investment, Technology and Enterprise Development
United Nations Office in Geneva
Palais des Nations
Room E-9123
CH-1211 Geneva 10
Switzerland
Fax: 41-22-907-0194

1. Name and address of respondent (optional):

_____
_____
_____

2. Which of the following best describes your area of work?

Government	☐	Public enterprise	☐
Private enterprise	☐	Academic or research Institution	☐
International organisation	☐	Media	☐
Not-for-profit organisation	☐	Other (specify) _____	

3. In which country do you work?

_____

4. What is your assessment of the contents of this publication?

Excellent	☐	Adequate	☐
Good	☐	Poor	☐

5. How useful is this publication to your work?

Very useful ☐   Of some use ☐   Irrelevant ☐

6. Please indicate the three things you liked best about this publication:

_____
_____
_____

7. Please indicate the three things you liked least about this publication:

_____
_____
_____

8. If you have read other publications of the UNCTD Division on Investment, Enterprise Development and Technology, what is your overall assessment of them?

    Consistently good   ☐   Usually good, but

                                              with some exceptions   ☐

    Generally mediocre   ☐   Poor   ☐

9. On the average, how useful are those publications to you in your work?

Very useful   ☐   Of some use   ☐   Irrelevant   ☐

10. Are you a regular recipient of Transnational Corporations (formerly The CTC Reporter), UNCTAD-DITE's tri-annual refereed journal?

        Yes   ☐   No   ☐

    If not, please check here if you would like to receive   a sample copy sent to the name and address you have given above   ☐

Printed at United Nations, Geneva
GE.06-50059–January 2006–3,295
Sales No. E.05.II.D.20

ISBN 92-1-112680-0
ISSN 1818-1465

UNCTAD/ITE/IIA/2005/1